U.S. Savings Bonds

A Comprehensive Guide for
Bond Owners and Financial Professionals

U.S. Savings Bonds

A Comprehensive Guide for
Bond Owners and Financial Professionals

Daniel J. Pederson

TSBI Publishing, Detroit, Michigan

To Anna Anderson, Mary Lou Parlato, and Ruth Schlesser, retirees who follow the ultimate example of a life devoted to serving others.

TSBI Publishing
P.O. Box 9249
Detroit, MI 48209
(313) 843-1910

Editor: Christina Bych
Cover Design: Gary Hoffman

Publisher's Cataloging in Publication (Prepared by Quality Books Inc.)

Pederson, Daniel J.
     U.S. savings bonds : a comprehensive guide for bond owners and financial professionals / Daniel J. Pederson -- 2nd ed. --
Detroit, MI : TSBI Pub., 1995.
     p. cm.
     Includes bibliographical references and index.
     Preassigned LCCN: 95-60754.
     ISBN 0-9643020-1-2

     1. Savings bonds--United States. 2. Government securities--United States   I. Title.

HG4936.P43 1995   332.63'23
                                   QBI95-20205

Printed in the United States of America
10 9 8 7 6 5 4 3 2

Disclaimer: While the author and publisher have made every effort to provide information which, at the time of publication, is as accurate and complete as possible in regard to the subject matter covered, it is acknowledged that mistakes, both in content and typography could exist. Current investment information should be obtained from the Department of Treasury, Bureau of the Public Debt, before making any decisions to buy, sell, reissue or exchange any U.S. Savings Bonds. This publication is sold with the understanding that the publisher is not engaged in rendering legal, tax, accounting and like services. If legal advice, tax advice or other expert assistance is required, the services of a professional in that field should be sought.

For purchasing information, including quantity discounts, contact:
TSBI Publishing (313) 843-1910.

Contents

Tables and Figures

Preface

Although most of this book was finished during the summer of 1994, the research unknowingly began on a bright spring morning in May 1986. I had been in the position of the Supervisor of the Savings Bond Division of the Federal Reserve Bank of Chicago, Detroit Branch, for a grand total of five weeks.

The area that I managed received 200 to 500 calls each day from the general public and financial institutions. The majority of these calls were channeled to the telephone answering unit, the customer service area of the division. At the time, one person handled the calls, with the overflow randomly dispersed throughout the division.

The man responsible for taking these calls left for a one-week vacation and, as the rookie supervisor, I had to determine who would "cover the phones." Since the number of calls that a person handled was not one of the significant activities tracked and measured, respect and enthusiasm for this job was low. Rather than pull someone from one of the "more important" activities of processing volumes of transactions, I, being naive, decided to cover the phones myself.

At the designated moment on Monday morning, the weekend recording was turned off and the fun began. That was the longest, most difficult week of my career at the Federal Reserve Bank. Call after call, the questions came: "Tell me.... Help me.... How do I...? When does this happen...? How does that work...? Does it matter if I...? Which form should I use to...?" This new supervisor came away with a profound sense of how much he did not know. But more important, the phone time allowed me to assess the knowledge base of my division, the resources that were available to answer questions, and the demands and expectations of the consumer.

In 1990, I left the Federal Reserve Bank to start The Savings Bond Informer, Inc., a company that provides detailed reports and information on United States Savings Bonds. Having worked closely with thousands of Bond owners and financial professionals for nine years, this work is a result of listening, learning, researching, and helping.

The following pages will address the major areas of information that Bond owners need to know. It is not an attempt to answer the question, "Are U.S. Savings Bonds the right investment for me?" That question can only be answered by assessing all the investment options available to each individual investor. This book will provide Bond owners and financial professionals with the tools necessary to evaluate Bond holdings, enabling them to begin any comparison process that they desire.

Very Important. May 1, 1995 the Treasury implemented a new set of rules for Series EE bonds purchased on or after that date. As you read this book, please be aware that until the year 2000 approximately 90+% of the Bonds outstanding had been purchased prior to May 1, 1995, and thus are governed by the "old" rules. While this text will fully describe the new rules and how they affect bond owners, there is considerable attention given to the old rules, because this is the largest group of bonds that are currently outstanding.

This book is not a government publication; however, materials published by the Treasury Department and the Internal Revenue Service have been incorporated. In addition, the tax chapter (Chapter 8) was extensively researched and compiled by Brent Dawes, CPA, manager at American Express Tax and Business Services. The perspective of a CPA resulted in numerous "Tax Tips" and "Tax Traps." All documents used or referred to have been listed in the Bibliography. The Glossary explains unfamiliar terms.

If I am not mistaken, this is not the kind of book that you will stay up until 3:00 a.m. reading because the story line is unrelenting. I am confident, though, that this book will meet your expectations as the most thorough guide available on the topic of U.S. Savings Bonds.

Acknowledgments

For the development of this book and The Savings Bond Informer, Inc., I am deeply grateful:

—To David Pederson, my brother, who urged me to write this book.

—To my associates at the FRB of Chicago, Detroit Branch. Especially my friend Robert Jones who picked May 1986 for a week of vacation and provided me with the opportunity to learn how important it is to service Savings Bond owners. He challenged me to learn something new each day. Also, Willie Mae Hall and Larry Pasden: Their hard work and professionalism have left a lasting impression; they always listened, helped, and provided invaluable counsel during my tenure at the FRB. And for my former staff in the Savings Bond Division who generously shared their Bond knowledge with me.

—To my outstanding associates at The Savings Bond Informer: Randy Bonser, Roxanne Brogden, Shanai Celina, Lydia Garcia, Marijane Grimaldo, Louise Paladino, Sue Konieczko, Paul Meriweather, and Nghi Anh Street-Tran, all of whom at various times held down the fort of business operations while I was out playing basketball, oops, I mean, working on this book. More important, for their dedication, and commitment to treating our clients with dignity and service that continues to "wow" them. For Nando Garcia and Melissa Lemuel whose contributions are a shining example of hard work.

—In addition, Randy Bonser, who created, edited, researched, edited, made calls, edited, wrote, edited, rewrote, and edited. Speaking of harnessing Niagara..his skills were critical to the production of this book.

—To my Seed Family, for investing, critiquing, and counsel that provided an important role in shaping the direction of our company. Hill House rules in golf. For Soda, to use a phrase from that first piece of impressive writing for our graduating class at Taylor, "Is this the apex of the triangle...?" From pedaling a bike across America, to serving in urban centers, a more faithful friend who can find? His world view inspires.

—To many friends for support, ideas, and encouragement. Greg Schupra's challenges have sharpened and pushed me (the "pushed me" part also applies to lunchtime basketball). He, Ray Frederick, and Jack and Theo Robinson have always believed. Dan Johanon provided countless pieces of practical advice in addition to offering his technical skills. (And, of equal importance, he helped me muster multiple excuses to have lunch.) Jim and Lisa Lochrie and Joel Manby gave special project assistance.

—To Brent Dawes. I have certainly gained a whole new appreciation for his ability to interpret language that includes "elections" that have nothing to do with voting, "nominees" that are not running for office, and a "cash basis" which is not how much change I have left after springing for pizza. Did a former politician create the tax language? Or did a tax man create the political process? His contributions to this book are tremendous.

—To Christina Bych, an exceptional editor and consultant. Her personal interest and professional approach brought an infant work to maturity. I was continually amazed at her ability to shape and rework this text. Gary Hoffman for an excellent cover design. I specifically picked someone out of state so he couldn't easily come and beat me up after the 23rd revision.

—To Dorothy Riley, for leading us to the right resources and providing us with the advice that not only got us started, but helped us stay on-track through to the completion of this project.

—To Bill Greenman. I admire his entrepreneurial accomplishments, have benefitted from his printing expertise, and see him as a real model of service. While more than occupied with his own business, he always makes the time to go the extra mile.

—Last and most important, to my family, especially Anna Marie, my wife, best friend, business partner, and greatest supporter. I am grateful for her advice when I asked for it and...even when I didn't (like the night she warned me not to press certain computer keys, but, hey, I don't need to ask for directions, so I pressed the keys and dumped this whole document. Thank goodness for backups and a wife that forgives). Without her, this book would never have happened. Ron and Anne VonGunten for always being willing to help in whatever capacity was needed, even if it meant driving for hours on short notice. A special thanks to Anne for working into the wee hours of the morning; she has a heart of gold. Vonnie Pederson for feedback, constant encouragement, and all the extras even in the midst of a busy schedule. Sever Pederson for enthusiasm, energy, and ideas, and always asking how it was going. Esther Marlow, for helping lay the foundation of our operation; we follow the professional legacy that she began. Dan Marlow, for hours of telecommunications consulting and ideas. Anna Anderson: Nike must have studied her life before they coined the phrase, "Just do it." Whatever it took, she stood ready and "just did it" over and over again; a tireless saint to all who know her, she kept the crew going.

_____
_____ Chapter 1

WHY A BOOK ON
U.S. SAVINGS BONDS?

▸ *Two Primary Misconceptions about U.S. Savings Bonds*
▸ *Lack of Information Leads to Costly Mistakes*
▸ *What You Can Expect from this Book*
▸ *What You Cannot Expect from this Book*
▸ *How to Use this Book*

> Americans now hold over $170 billion in Savings Bonds...
> and each year 14 million people buy more, making them
> the world's most widely held security.
> —"U.S. Savings Bonds, 1994 Campaign: Visions of
> America," NYNEX Corporation.

Over 55 million Americans own U.S. Savings Bonds. Yet, up to now, no one has made a concerted effort to provide a comprehensive, consumer-friendly guide, one designed to help Bond owners and financial professionals understand and evaluate this investment. This book will aid in making the crucial decisions that ultimately can result in maximizing the value of the owner's Bond holdings.

The information presented is *not* an attempt to convince the reader to buy more Bonds or to sell Bonds already owned, rather the focus is on educating Bond owners so that they may better handle the investment they already have. It could mean a difference of thousands of dollars.

Two Primary Misconceptions about U.S. Savings Bonds

U.S. Savings Bonds are familiar to us and have been so for some time. Americans started purchasing Series E Bonds in the 1940s. These Bonds are fondly remembered as "War Bonds," because many people bought them to support our country during World War II. Understanding them has always seemed like a simple matter: *Everybody knows about U.S. Savings Bonds, right?* The typical pattern has been to collect Bonds over the years and then to redeem them when it is time to make that big purchase. Unfortunately, this has often led to costly mistakes.

Misconception #1: *U.S. Savings Bonds Are a Simple Investment*

The concept that Savings Bonds are a simple investment is derived from the fact that they are easy to purchase. They can be bought at thousands of banks across the country or through a Payroll Savings Plan at work. However, they are not as simple as meets the eye.

Each Bond carries a unique set of information specific to that Bond alone. This includes interest rates (two of them), timing issues, maturity dates, values, and accrued interest. Knowing the unique information that applies to each one of your Bonds can make a significant difference in the return on your investment. Not knowing can mean forfeiting hundreds or in some cases, thousands of dollars.

Misconception #2: *Everyone Knows How Savings Bonds Work*

The author has conducted hundreds of Savings Bond seminars for bankers, attorneys, accountants, financial planners, brokers, and Bond owners. One of the first questions posed to the participants is the most basic and common question about Bonds: How long does it take a Bond that was purchased in 1994 to reach face value, at the guaranteed interest rate? In every group there are at least three or four different answers, often as many as six or seven.

The confusion surrounding this most basic question would indicate that there is a greater amount of misunderstanding on the more detailed and technical questions. In a recent survey of 400 banks, only 38% answered the question correctly. Indeed, a bank in Florida reported that Bonds reach face value in two years, which would mean that the

Bonds would have to pay interest at a rate of 36%. Another bank indicated that it takes thirty years for a Bond to reach face value and, as a result, the interest rate would have to be under 2½%.

The reason for such an expanse of misinformation is that Savings Bonds operate according to different rules depending on their type (series), and when they were purchased. For example, two Series E Bonds with the same face value, but purchased at different times, can come under different rules (which, in turn, lead to different rates of interest and strategic timing considerations). Yet, many people treat Bonds as though they are all the same.

One of the most significant changes in the Bond program occurred May 1, 1995. This introduced a whole new set of rules for Series EE Bonds purchased on or after that date.

Savings Bonds are certainly not a "simple investment." Furthermore, the perception that everyone knows how they work has led to a mindset that has often prevented Bond owners from seeking the critical information that they need in order to be knowledgeable about their Bonds.

Lack of Information
Leads to Costly Mistakes

After every seminar, a line quickly forms with people ready to tell the author "their Savings Bond story." Often the tale involves a financial mistake brought on by the advice of a misinformed person:

- A man redeemed all of his Bonds right before retirement, during the year when he was in the highest income bracket of his lifetime. He did not realize that all the interest income from the redeemed Bonds would be reported in that calendar year.

- A woman read a publication that advocated cashing in her Bonds that had reached face value to purchase new Bonds under the new rules. Many of her Bonds were still earning rates of 7.5% under the old rules, while the new rules would have netted her substantially less.

- A woman recently widowed was advised to cash all of her Bonds; she later learned that her Bonds would have continued to earn interest for an additional eight years.

- A father purchased an EE Bond for its educational feature only to discover that he may not meet the criteria to qualify for the tax-free status.

- A couple needed money for a down payment on a new home and so randomly cashed 50 of their 100 Bonds. If they had applied the principles of selective redemption, they would have had an additional $1,000 to $2,000 to use toward the purchase.

- A financial planner learned that over $50,000 of his client's $240,000 Bond holdings had stopped earning interest over five years ago.

- When advising a customer on how to remove the first-named living owner from a Bond, a banker did not counsel the new recipient on tax issues. Subsequently, the new owner declared Bond interest that had already been declared at the time of reissue: a double taxation problem.

- An accountant did not know that Bonds do not automatically receive a stepped-up basis.

Unfortunately, the same stories are told over and over again. Sadder yet is the fact that many more people are in these situations, making the same mistakes.

It is our desire that by sharing these stories and by providing the much needed information that these Bond owners lacked, you will not be left with your own tale of woe. Instead, whether you choose to cash, exchange, or hold your Bonds, your choice will be based on facts.

What You Can Expect from this Book

U.S. Savings Bonds are a do-it-yourself proposition. Have you ever received a statement containing the precise details for each of your Bonds? Statements are sent for savings accounts, checking accounts, and mutual fund accounts. There was no such instrument available for U.S. Savings Bonds until the author created one in 1990. Once you invest in Savings Bonds, it is up to you to ask the right questions and find the right source for answers. After reading this book, or the chapters that apply to your situation, you will have a better idea of what questions to ask. In most cases, the answers will be provided; on the rare occasion that they are not, an appropriate resource will be given.

More specifically, this book will enable you to maximize your investment in U.S. Savings Bonds in two ways. The first is by building your understanding of how Savings Bonds work. For example, in the following chapters Bond owners will find full explanations of:

✓ Interest Rates:
—The guaranteed rate
—The market-based rates (short-term and long-term)

✓ Timing Issues:
—When Bonds increase in value
—When they enter an extended maturity
—When they stop earning interest

✓ Maturity Periods:
—Why the term "maturity" is used in three different ways
—What original maturity, extended maturity, and final maturity mean

✓ Tax Issues:
—The discrepancy between IRS rules and the reporting system for interest income
—The educational feature of the Series EE Bond

✓ Comparison of Old Rules and New Rules:
—Summary of each set of rules
—What Bond owners gain and what they have lost
—Which Bonds are affected by which set of rules

Second, step-by-step instructions are provided on how to track your investment and how to organize and keep important records on your Bonds. Tables and figures, usually found at the end of the chapter, illustrate key concepts and provide examples of what to do.

Several areas are especially noteworthy, such as: four ways Savings Bonds are **double taxed**; an introduction to the concept of **selective redemption**; and the results from a **survey of 400 banks** regarding the Savings Bond information they provide to the public.

What You Cannot Expect from this Book

This is not a book about municipal bonds, corporate bonds, bond mutual funds, Treasury Bills, Treasury Notes, or Treasury Bonds. There are plenty of comprehensive publications available on these topics. This book will only deal with issues directly related to U.S. Savings Bonds: Series E, EE, H, HH, and Savings Notes (SN).

This book is not a government publication. Several government publications are used as reference materials and are noted in the Bibliography.

Finally, you will not find advice on whether or not to invest in Savings Bonds or what to do with your interest earnings upon redemption of your Bonds. While the pros and cons of making certain decisions are sometimes given for your consideration, this job is best left to you or someone, such as a financial professional, who is familiar with your overall financial picture.

How to Use this Book

This book can be used as a guide or as a reference. As a guide, it explains some of the most technical information in an easy-to-understand manner. When called for, it will take you step-by-step through various processes. As a reference manual, it has been organized to provide quick and easy access to the information you seek. The Contents provides not only chapter titles, but also the subheadings which describe the main points of each chapter. These subheadings are repeated at the beginning of each chapter; a quick browse will likely direct you to the proper section within a given chapter. The Glossary provides definitions of Bond-related terms and phrases. (Check here first should you come across something unfamiliar.) The Index lists Savings Bond activities and terms by name so the page number can be quickly located. Chapter 16 provides a brief summary of the content of this book in a helpful question-and-answer format.

In an attempt to make the information easy to follow, you will find that some areas are repetitious. Often a piece of data will apply to several different issues. Rather than refer you to other chapters, which creates time-consuming page turning, that material is summarized for immediate use, followed by directions to more detailed information on the topic.

There is a wealth of information in Chapter 17, "U.S. Savings Bond Resources." It covers both government and nongovernment agencies that provide a variety of Savings Bond services. It also lists the various forms needed to complete Savings Bond transactions and where to obtain them. The directory of phone numbers and addresses will lead you to any additional help you may need.

Millions of Americans have relied on U.S. Savings Bonds as a way to save and invest. Whether you own Bonds or work with Bond owners, the following pages will provide you with the opportunity to understand and manage a Savings Bond investment.

Chapter 2

BANKS AND BONDS:
THE UNTOLD STORY

▸ *U.S. Savings Bonds Are Not a Bank Product*
▸ *The Changing Relationship between Banks and Bonds*
▸ *Evaluation of Bank Services: The Good, The Bad, and The Ugly*
▸ *How to Determine the Level of Service Your Bank Provides*

> Few other industries have been asked by the government to take actions adverse to their own interests in the way the banks have been exhorted to sell U.S. Savings Bonds through the years.
>
> —Paul S. Nadler, "Uncle Sam Out of Line,"
> *Banker's Monthly* (November 1992), p. 8.

If you own U.S. Saving Bonds, you probably bought them at your local bank or through a Payroll Savings Plan. Because banks handle a variety of financial products and services, Bond owners often assume that the bank is knowledgeable about Bonds. As you will see, this assumption could prove to be very costly.

U.S. Savings Bonds Are Not a Bank Product

U.S. Savings Bonds are a product of the federal government. They are not, nor have they ever been, a product created and fully supported by the banks. Because Bonds are not a bank product, financial institutions rely on information from the government when informing the public about them.

Banks receive a small fee for handling the Bond purchase application and for redeeming Bonds. They do not receive money for advising individuals regarding Bond holdings. Most banks would not describe Bonds as a money-maker. They handle Bonds as a courtesy to prevent customers from moving to another bank (and taking their money with them). As a result, most banks do not put a high priority on training their personnel in answering questions on U.S. Savings Bond timing and interest rate issues. Training dollars are typically spent on bank products more likely to generate substantial revenue.

The Changing Relationship between Banks and Bonds

Before you get angry at your bank, consider this: How would you feel if you were selling a product that not only competed with your own product line, but was twice as good as your product, and yet left you with no profit? That was the unenviable position in which banks found themselves during 1992: Bonds had a guaranteed rate of 6% while savings accounts, along with some Certificates of Deposit (CDs), were struggling to reach 3%. Needless to say, the smart bankers were not excited to see an all-time high of $17.6 billion in Savings Bond sales. Why? Many buyers were shifting their money from CDs into Savings Bonds; that is, they were taking money out of bank products and investing it in a government product. And the banks had to help them do this.

In the last few years, The Savings Bond Informer, Inc. has received an increasing number of calls from people saying, "My bank no longer deals with Savings Bonds." This is particularly true of clients on the West Coast and, most recently, clients in eastern Pennsylvania. Given that Savings Bonds compete for the dollars of bank customers, it is not surprising that some banks are decreasing their level of service related to Bonds.

When dealing with your bank on Savings Bond issues, there are two questions to be concerned with:
- ✓ What level of service do they provide?
- ✓ Will they put their answers in writing?

Evaluation of Bank Services: The Good, The Bad, and The Ugly

The Good

Many banks act as a point of sale for the purchase of Bonds and a point of redemption for the cashing of Bonds. For the most part, banks do a good job identifying what a Bond is worth. They have standardized tables that provide redemption values. In fact, in a recent survey, many bank tellers would give the value of a Bond in response to questions about interest rates or timing issues. The reason for this is that they are generally good at valuing Savings Bonds. However, as with any money matter, it makes good sense to double check the calculations yourself, whenever possible. A financial planner recently called with the following story.

I was working on a case for an estate settlement. The law firm needed Bonds evaluated, so I used your service to provide a report for them. Today they called to tell me they had cashed some of the Bonds. There was one problem, though: they received $1,000 less than they thought they should have. After checking your report, they called the bank and asked them to recheck their figures. Sure enough, the bank amount was wrong. The bank apologized several times for their error. The bottom line is that had we not had the report, we would not have known we were being shorted.

Because he was an informed consumer, the client got the money due him the same day.

Watch out, though. If a bank overpays you, an unpleasant surprise may be forthcoming. Another financial planner reported that a client had been contacted several months after redeeming some Bonds. The bank claimed overpayment and requested that the money be returned.

Note: The government does not double check every Bond transaction. They check batch totals. A batch total is a group of Bonds combined together. Settlements on a price difference are not made directly with the Bond owner. The government adjusts large differences with financial institutions; it is the responsibility of the financial institution to refund or seek payment from a Bond owner in the event of an over- or underpayment. Bond owners should verify that they have received the correct amount upon redemption of their Bonds. **Suggestion:** To confirm your Bonds' worth, obtain a detailed statement or the redemption tables. See Chapter 17, "U.S. Savings Bond Resources," and Chapter 6, "Tracking Your Investment," for more information.

The Bad

You, as a Bond owner, deserve and must have accurate information. The reason inaccurate information exists is that bank tellers, who are not analysts, act as consultants on Bonds. Note the following example.

A man went into a bank in Michigan with E Bonds he had purchased in the 1970s. He asked the teller what he should do. After consulting her charts, she informed him that the Bonds were no longer earning interest and that he should redeem them all. He followed her advice and liquidated all of his Bonds from the 70s that he had purchased through payroll deduction.

Why was this a disaster? First, his Bonds had not stopped earning interest: The teller had given him incorrect information. His Bonds would have continued to earn interest until after the year 2000. Second, when he redeemed the Bonds, he had to declare *all* the interest income that year. The tragedy was that this man was two years from retirement and so was in *the highest income bracket of his lifetime.* Third, many of his Bonds had been earning attractive rates of 7.5%. Unfortunately, this man did not get any of the teller's information in writing. He was understandably enraged by his experience.

Never trust verbal information about interest rates and timing issues for your Bonds. If you choose to rely upon your bank, ask that all the information they give you be put into writing, including the name of the person with whom you spoke. Also record the date and location of your inquiry.

The Ugly

Assume you ask a bank teller a question about what interest rates your Bonds are earning. What is the likelihood of getting someone who is knowledgeable about Bonds and can produce the correct answer? Our research indicates that less than one out of ten bank personnel can accurately answer Bond questions. Yet, approximately nine out of ten bank representatives will either confidently give inaccurate answers or admit they "don't know." Going to the next level of management does not ensure accuracy, either; those in upper management deal with Savings Bonds even less frequently.

So, what happens to Jane Q. Public, the Bond owner? She walks away believing what she has been told. Someday Jane will act on the information she was given and probably never realize that she did not receive the maximum potential return on her Bond investment.

How to Determine the Level of Service Your Bank Provides

Repeated complaints from Bond owners led The Savings Bond Informer to design and conduct extensive surveys of banks regarding the Savings Bond information they provide to the public.

Between April 15, 1994, and August 15, 1994, over 400 banks in ten states (New York, California, Florida, Michigan, Arizona, Illinois, Indiana, Wisconsin, Iowa, and Texas) were contacted by phone. The initial request was "I have some questions about U.S. Savings Bonds. Do you have someone who can assist me?" Often the result was several transfers and minutes on hold before the (presumably) most experienced and available person on the subject would take the call.

Five questions were asked. A correct answer was received 23% of the time. An incorrect answer was received 42% of the time. The bank representative said, "I don't know," 35% of the time.

Two of the questions focused on the interest rates and timing issues for older Bonds. Only 8% of the answers to these questions were correct. Over 90% of the banks surveyed did not or could not give accurate interest rate and timing issue information for an older Bond. To their credit, 48% of the banks admitted they did not know. However, 44% of the banks answered boldly and inaccurately.

How many banks answered all the questions correctly? How many banks could you rely on to provide accurate answers to Savings Bond questions? In this survey of 400 banks, only four banks answered all five questions correctly. The math is not difficult here: Exactly 1% of the banks surveyed knew the correct answer to each question.

Some of the more dramatic, and woefully wrong, answers were so frightening that they deserve to be printed. Here are the top ten losing responses.

Question: *How long will it take a Bond purchased today (1994) to reach face value, at the current guaranteed interest rate?*

1. "Thirty years, or fifteen years."
2. "Five years"
3. "Two years"
4. "Twenty-five to thirty years"

Answer: *Eighteen years.*

Question: *Is the interest on a Bond purchased in January of 1963 compounded? If yes, is it daily, monthly, quarterly, semi-annually, or annually?*

1. "Monthly" (most common response)
2. "Kinda like quarterly, yet it's not"
3. "Calculated monthly, paid quarterly"
4. "Doesn't matter. Very complicated, based on when you bought it, how much you paid, and a lot of other factors"

Answer: *Compounded semi-annually.*

Two additional responses were noteworthy:

1. One person said that a Bond purchased in January 1963 is currently earning 18% interest. (This certainly beats the savings account rate that bank is offering.)
2. Another person said this same Bond would never stop earning interest. What a deal!

By now you get the point.

The conscientious bank employees said, "I don't know." This does not help you, the Bond owner, but neither does it hurt you. The damaging answers were from those people who *confidently* gave wrong information.

The bank employees who answered, "I don't know," however, often suggested an inadequate alternative. They would say, "Call this number and they will help you, 1-800-USBONDS." The caller, in turn, would ask, "Is there a person on that line who will address my questions?" The consistent response was, "Yes." In fact, that 800 number carries a recorded message that promotes the sale of new Bonds. There is no opportunity to ask a specific question.

Conclusion: Seventy-seven percent of the 2,000 questions asked were answered incorrectly or with "I don't know."

A Test For Your Bank Teller

Questions:

1. *Is interest compounded for Bonds purchased in the 1970s or 1980s? If so, is it daily, monthly, quarterly, semi-annually, or annually?*

2. *What is the current guaranteed interest rate for a Bond purchased January 1978? How long is that rate in effect?*

3. *Is there a specific month or months that would be best to cash a Bond dated November 1973?*

Answers:

1. The interest on these Bonds accrues and is compounded semi-annually. Why is this important? If you cash your Bond even one day before a semi-annual increase, you will forfeit up to six months of interest.

2. This Bond has a current guaranteed rate of 6% which will be in effect until January 2003. Why is this important? Knowing specific interest rates, and how long those rates are good, will help you make hold or sell decisions.

3. Yes. For a Bond purchased November 1973, the months of increase are September and March. Why is this important? If your teller says it does not matter when you cash your Bond, he or she obviously does not understand how Bonds work.

   In conclusion, there are four points of action to take when seeking advice on your Bond holdings.

   1. Make sure you are dealing with someone who is knowledgeable.
   2. Get the facts in writing.
   3. Get the name of the person with whom you are dealing.
   4. Always recheck transactions.

Remember, free information is not a bargain unless it is correct.

Chapter 3

UNDERSTANDING INTEREST RATES
a.k.a. Harnessing Niagara Falls

- ▸ *Why Bond Owners Need to Know Interest Rates*
- ▸ *Why All the Confusion?*
- ▸ *Common Misconceptions*
- ▸ *How Interest Rates Are Determined*
  - —*The Old Rules*
    - • *The Guaranteed Rate*
    - • *The Market-Based Variable Rate*
  - —*The New Rules*
    - • *Short-Term Market Rate*
    - • *Long-Term Market Rate*
- ▸ *When Will the Interest Rates Change?*

There is more confusion over U.S. Savings Bond interest rates than there is water over Niagara Falls. Savings Bonds are often referred to as a "simple investment product." That reference is accurate if one is referring to the relative ease of purchase and the uncomplicated purchase pricing structure. (For EE Bonds, for example, you pay half of the face value, no commissions, no hidden fees.) However, those who

15

say that the interest rates are "all the same" do not understand Savings Bonds.

Why Bond Owners Need to Know Interest Rates

The biggest reason why this knowledge is critical is that *not knowing may result in a financial loss*. Consider this example:

John Smith has purchased Savings Bonds for the last twenty years. He has a combination of over 100 E and EE Bonds. He needs to cash some Bonds for a down payment on a car. John figures that about twenty Bonds would get him the $10,000 he needs. Which Bonds should he cash? Looking at the Bonds provides no clue as to their interest rates. John decides to take the oldest twenty and cash them.

The Mistake: Several of the Bonds John picked had guaranteed rates of 7.5% and 6.0%, while others that he chose to keep had a guaranteed rate of 4%. This simple decision will cost John about $200 to $350 annually for every $10,000 of Bonds he owns.

Knowing the specific interest rates of your Bonds will help you get the maximum financial benefit from your investment.

Why All the Confusion?

Because it just isn't easy.... If it's any comfort, you will not be alone when you say "I can't believe that is the way Savings Bonds work." Different rules govern different Bonds. The issue date of a Bond will determine which set of rules and interest rate(s) affect it. Prior to engaging in a discussion on this topic, background is necessary.

Until 1982 the Savings Bond program enjoyed a monogamous relationship with the interest rate. That is, there was only one type of interest rate—the guaranteed (fixed) interest rate. Bonds had different guaranteed rates assigned to them depending on the purchase date and the specific maturity period they were in at that time. (For more on maturity periods, see Chapter 4.) Consequently, knowing what your Bond was earning at any point in time was based on that one rate.

In 1982 the government introduced the market-based variable interest rate to the Savings Bond Program. This rate was designed to make Bonds more competitive and attractive. Each Bond now has an upside potential: that is, it can earn an interest rate above the guaranteed interest rate if the Bond is held five years or longer. Thus, the government calculates two values for each Series E, EE or SN held for at least five years after November 1982: one based on the guaranteed rates and one based on the variable rates. The Bond would automatically receive the rate that produced the highest redemption value for a given redemption period. A complete illustration and explanation of this feature is included in Table 3.4.

In May 1995 the government both simplified and complicated this discussion on interest rates. They simplified interest rate structures by changing the rules so that only one interest rate will apply at any given point in time to Series EE Bonds issued on or after May 1, 1995. The complication is that most Bond owners have Bonds governed by the old set of rules. As they purchase Bonds under the new rules, they will need to know both the old *and* the new rules in order to understand and track their Savings Bond investment.

Throughout the remainder of this book you will see reference to the "Old Rules" and the "New Rules." The "Old Rules" apply to Series E, EE, or Savings Notes purchased prior to May 1, 1995. The "New Rules" apply only to Series EE Bonds purchased on or after May 1, 1995.

Common Misconceptions

all our bonds are determined by "old rules"

Examining some of the most common misunderstandings about interest rates may be useful in learning the "real story."

Misconception #1: *All Series E and EE Bonds earn the same rate of interest.*

No. Each Bond can have a unique guaranteed and market-based average variable interest rate if purchased prior to May 1, 1995. The rate for any given Bond is determined by the issue date of that Bond.

If purchased on or after May 1, 1995, a Series EE Bond receives a new short-term market rate every six months for the first five years. After five years the Bond receives a new long-term market rate every six months.

Misconception #2: *The interest rate that is quoted when you buy the Bond is good for the life of the Bond.*

No. "Old Rules": The guaranteed rate that is in effect when you buy an E, EE, or SN is the minimum rate you can receive during the original maturity period, i.e., the time period it will take for a Bond to reach face value at the guaranteed interest rate in effect at the time of purchase. (Exceptions apply to Series EE Bonds less than five years old and purchased prior to March 1, 1993.) However, a Bond will continue to earn interest well after the original maturity period; the guaranteed rate that was in effect when you purchased the Bond can change each time the Bond enters an extended maturity period.

"New Rules": When you buy a Series EE Bond, the short-term market rate in effect will impact your Bond for the first six months only. A new short-term market rate will be published every six months and that rate will impact your Bond for the next six month period. The first rate published when you purchase a Bond has no bearing on the future rates that will impact your Bond.

Misconception #3: *Older Bonds have lower interest rates than newer Bonds.*

No. Older Bonds can carry guaranteed rates as high as 7.5%. Bonds purchased as recently as March 1993 to April 1995 have guaranteed rates as low as 4%. The interest rates vary from Bond to Bond.

Misconception #4: *Newer Bonds have lower interest rates than older Bonds.*

A Bond purchased in the early 1990s may have a guaranteed rate of 6% (if held for five years), while an older Bond may have recently entered an extended maturity period at a guaranteed rate of only 4%. The interest rates vary from Bond to Bond. (The extended maturity period is the ten-year period that follows the completion of an original maturity period or a previous extended maturity period. It can be less than ten years if it is the last extended maturity period prior to the Bond reaching final maturity.)

Misconception #5: *The market-based variable rate that is published every May and November is the real rate on my Bonds.*

"Old Rules": **No**. The individual rate published each May and November has *no significance by itself*. This is not the rate your Bonds are earning. More on this later in this chapter.

"New Rules": **Yes**. Only for Series EE Bonds purchased after April 30, 1995. The short-term individual rate published each May and November will impact your Bond for the following six-month period if your Bond is less than five years old. The first time the long-term rate will impact any Bond under the new rules is May/2000. Once your Bond is five years or older, then the long-term market rate will be assigned to your Bond for the next six-month period.

Misconception #6: *The interest rate my bank teller quotes me is what my Bonds will earn.*

Not necessarily. You will receive whatever interest rates apply to your Bonds based on the federal government's interest rates and guidelines—regardless of any number a bank teller quotes you.

Misconception #7: *Interest is compounded daily, like my savings account.*

No. For Series EE Bonds over thirty months old and purchased prior to March 1, 1993, and for Series E and SN, the interest accrues and is compounded semi-annually. For a Series EE Bond purchased between March 1, 1993, and April 30, 1995, the increase is monthly for the first five years; however, the interest is still compounded semi-annually. For Series EE Bonds purchased May 1, 1995, and after, the interest accrues and is compounded semi-annually.

How Interest Rates Are Determined: "The Old Rules"

A primary source of confusion is that very few people understand that the government has established two interest rates for every Bond—Series E, EE, and SN—purchased prior to May 1, 1995. These two rates are called the guaranteed interest rate and the average market-based rate (also referred to as the variable interest rate).

To further complicate matters, the rate that receives the most attention from press releases put out by the federal government—and consequently, the media and the public—is the *individual* long-term market-based rate for a given six-month period. This rate is published every May and November. The *individual* long-term market-based variable rate is insignificant by itself for Bonds purchased prior to May 1, 1995. It only has importance to a Bond owner in relationship to all the other *individual* long-term market-based variable rates that are published over the life of a Bond which, when combined, make up the *average* market-based rate.

The Guaranteed Rate

Take a moment to answer a one-question quiz:

How long does it take a Bond with a guaranteed interest rate of 4% to reach face value?

    A. Seven years
    B. Ten years
    C. Twelve years
    D. Eighteen years
    E. Thirty years

Answer: *D. Eighteen years*. The Bond can reach face value in less than eighteen years if the market-based average variable interest rate exceeds 4%. Even if the Bond reaches face value in less than eighteen years, however, the original maturity period is still fixed at eighteen years.

At seminars that the author has conducted, fewer than 25% of the participants answer this question correctly. In our survey of 400 banks (described in Chapter 2) the question was answered correctly 38% of the time (and this was the highest percentage of correct answers for any of the survey questions). Some of the most damaging incorrect answers were two years (which would mean the Bond would be paying 36%) and seven years (the Bond would have to pay over 10% interest).

Under the "Old Rules," two important figures are assigned to a Bond upon issuance.

    1. The guaranteed interest rate
    2. The original maturity period

The *guaranteed interest rate* is the minimum rate that the Bond will yield until the end of the *original maturity period*. The original maturity period is revealed by the answer to the question, "How long will it take my Bond to reach face value at the guaranteed interest rate of ...X percent?" In this case, the original maturity period is eighteen years based on the guaranteed rate of 4%. (See Chapter 4 for a further explanation of maturity periods.)

The guaranteed rate assigned to your Bond at purchase is *not* in effect for the life of the Bond. This is a particular surprise and disappointment to Bond holders who bought in the mid-1980s at 7.5%. They thought that rate would be good for as long as the Bond was held. In reality, those Bond holders are guaranteed 7.5% for the original maturity period only (ten years, in this case).

The guaranteed rate that is assigned to your Bond, based on the purchase date, is good until your Bond reaches the end of the original maturity period. For Series E and EE Bonds, original maturity periods vary from five to eighteen years, depending on the issue date. After that time, the Bond enters an *extension period* of ten years. A new guaranteed rate will be in effect for the ten-year extension. The original maturity period for Savings Notes is four years, six months.

For example, assume in the following illustration that the Bond will be held to *final maturity*—in this case, thirty years from the date of purchase—when the Bond stops earning interest. A Series EE Bond purchased in July 1984 has a guaranteed rate of 7.5% and an original maturity period of ten years. In July 1994, the Bond entered its first ten-year extended maturity period. The guaranteed rate for that Bond during this first *extended maturity period* dropped to 4%. Why?

Bonds are assigned the guaranteed rate in effect on the date they enter into a new extension period. As of July 1994, the guaranteed rate was 4%. This Bond will now carry that 4% rate until July 2004. In July 2004, the Bond will enter its last extension of ten years (the total life of this Bond is thirty years). The guaranteed rate for the last ten years will be whatever the guaranteed rate is as of July 2004. That final guaranteed rate will stay with the Bond until final maturity in July 2014.

The Market-Based Variable Rate

> The market-based interest rate is set at 85 percent of the average yield, during the time the Bonds are held, of marketable Treasury securities with five years remaining to maturity.
>
> —U.S. Department of the Treasury, Bureau of the Public Debt, U.S. Savings Bond Division, "Savings Bond Buyer's Guide: 1993-1994," Pubn. SBD-2085.

The rates published every May and November are calculated on the previous six months' data for marketable Treasury securities with five years remaining to maturity. The published rate on May 1, 1994, was 4.7%. This was the first semi-annual rate for Bonds purchased from May 1, 1994, to October 31, 1994. *This is not the rate these Bonds are currently earning.* (It will be easier to follow which interest rate impacts Bonds that are purchased under the "New Rules." The rate that is published will in fact be the actual rate your Bond will earn for the next six-month period.)

The difference between an *individual* market-based rate and the *average* of the market-based rates can be illustrated this way. A recent caller named Joan asked, "I bought Bonds in the 1980s at 11+%. I know they are still earning that interest, but for how long?" How did Joan arrive at the inaccurate conclusion that her Bonds were earning 11%? Because the first individual rate published for her Bonds was 11.09%. However, she never earned 11.09% because that number became part of an average once her Bonds were held five years. Examine Table 3.2 for a comparison of individual market-based rates and the average of the market-based rates for a given time period.

The market-based variable rate program generated enthusiasm when the rate of 11.09% was announced with the introduction of the program in November 1982.

Joan thought she was buying a Bond paying 11.09% but she was not. First, she would have to hold her Bond at least five years from the date of purchase to be eligible for the market-based variable rate program. If you redeem a Bond in less than five years, the variable rate program has absolutely no impact on your Bond. Second, all the rates published during the holding period of your Bond (five years or longer) are *averaged*. This average is then rounded to the nearest quarter or hundredth (depending on issue date and/or the date the Bond may have entered an extension). This rounded average is used to calculate a value for the Bond based on the average variable rates.

As you can see, Joan *never* received over 11% on her Bond. In fact, her current value is about equal under both interest rate structures. Why? In this case, the value based on the guaranteed rate of 7.5% over the first ten years and 6% in the Bond's current extension is virtually equal to the value using the *average* variable rate of 7.18% (average variable rate as of May 1, 1995) over the life of the Bond.

What is the bottom line? The significant number in the market-based variable rate program is the *average* variable rate of the specific Bonds you hold. One thing you can determine from the *individual* variable rate published every May and November is this: If the individual rate published is higher than your average, it will push the average up; if the individual rate published is lower than your average, it will pull the average down.

During a 1994 TV interview, the author mentioned that the guaranteed rate for Bonds purchased that day was 4%, even if they were held for only one, two, or three years. Following the broadcast, an angry Bond owner called in: "Bonds are paying 4.7% right now, the new rate was just announced this week!" This person did not understand that he was not getting "4.7% right now."

To qualify for the average variable interest rate, you must hold your Bonds for at least five years. During this time, all of the individual variable rates published would be averaged. If this average variable rate produces a Bond value greater than the value produced from the guaranteed rate (4%), then you would receive the average variable rate.

Bonds purchased with a guaranteed rate of 4% (March 1, 1993, to April 30, 1995) will likely see a significant jump in value once held five years. Why? Up to the four-year, eleven-month mark, the Bond value is based on a guaranteed rate of 4%. Once held five years, the average of the long-term variable rates published over the life of the Bond will be taken back to date of purchase and compounded forward (if the average is greater than 4%). On a Bond purchased March 1, 1993, there have been six rates published as of May 1995, and the average of those six rates is 5.17%. Four more rates will be added to the average by the time that Bond reaches five years old. However, if the remaining rates are close to the average, a jump in the interest rate of over 1.15% will be applied to the Bond retroactive to date of purchase.

As you can see from Table 3.2, in only two of sixteen times (sixteen because only Bonds five years old were counted) is the average variable rate higher than the first published variable rate. This is an historic view and one that has been affected by falling interest rates until May/1994. An additional table on the market-based rate is provided in Chapter 6 (Table 6.4).

An economy that produces rising interest rates over a long period of time could easily create an average variable rate that is higher than the first published variable rate. For example: A Bond purchased November 1993 was assigned a first variable rate of 4.25%. The second variable rate assigned to this Bond was 4.7%. The third rate was 5.92% and the fourth rate 6.31%. This Bond must be held five years to be eligible for the average of the variable rates. The first four rates average 5.3%. If that average held until the fifth year, that rate would then be retroactive to date of purchase. As you can see the average rate of 5.3% is much more attractive than the initial rate of 4.25%.

So, next May or November, when all the newspapers publish the press releases promoting the new individual variable rate system, you will be able to anticipate the forecast. Some writers will inaccurately say, "This is the new rate for all Bonds held today," but you will know better. Only the long-term variable rate will apply to Bonds purchased prior to May 1, 1995, and that long-term rate will become part of an average that may or may not impact your Bond. For further discussion on the application of the rates to your specific Bonds, see Chapter 6, "Tracking Your Investment."

A wise decision is always based in knowledge, knowing the "whole story." Understanding these interest rate issues will enable you to get the facts and better manage your financial resources.

Summary of the "Old Rules": The ultimate value of your Bond will never be less than the value produced by applying the guaranteed rates that have been in effect during the life of your Bond. Examine Table 3.3 for the guaranteed rates in effect as of May 1995.

The government actually tracks and calculates two values for every Bond over five years old. One value is based on the guaranteed rates in effect for that Bond and a different value is based on the average variable interest rate in effect for that Bond. As a Bond owner you automatically receive the rate(s) that produces the highest redemption value for a given redemption period. In some cases with older Bonds, even though the average variable rate may be higher than the guaranteed rate in the current maturity period, the guaranteed rate can be the rate that is producing the higher redemption value. Why? Previous guaranteed rates on that Bond can be as high as 7.5% to 8.5%. The average variable rate has a retroactive feature. When current individual variable rates that are below the average are published, they pull the average down.

If you would like to really dig into an example with more detail, see Table 3.4 and the accompanying explanation.

How Interest Rates Are Determined: "The New Rules"

The amount of space needed to describe the new rules is not even half of that needed for the old rules. Why? Because the new rules are easier to understand. In fact, many Bond owners will think that this is the way the program has always calculated interest.

"New Rules"

1. There is no guaranteed rate. A Bond is assigned only one rate at any given point in time.
2. There is no retroactive feature attached to any of the market-based rates.
3. What you see is what you get.

True enough, the government did save a tidy sum by changing the rules (see Chapter 15, which compares the Old Rules to the New Rules). Yet the simplicity of the new rules allow Bond owners to more readily understand and evaluate their Savings Bond investment.

Short-Term Market Rate

The short-term market rate is determined by taking 85% of the average of the six-month Treasury Bill yields for the three months prior to May and November. Don't worry, you don't have to do the calculations. The short-term rate is calculated and published by the Savings Bond program every May and November. The short-term rate is the only rate that will apply to a Bond the first five years.

Example: A Bond owner purchased a Bond May 1, 1995. This Bond will increase in value every May and November. Assume that the following table of short-term rates is published over the first five years:

Table 3.1

Fictitious Illustration of Short-Term Rates

Date Rate would be Published	Hypothetical Short-term Rate (for illustrative purpose only)
May/1995	5.25 short-term (s.t.) rate
November/1995	5.5 s.t
May/1996	5.9 s.t
November/1996	5.3 s.t
May/1997	4.6 s.t
November/1997	4.2 s.t.
May/1998	3.9 s.t.
November/1998	4.4 s.t.
May/1999	5.2 s.t.
November/1999	5.1 s.t.
May/2000	5.9 long-term (l.t.)

The data in this table is entirely fictitious. It's only purpose
is to provide information for the example below.

Example Only: On November 1, 1995, this Bond will be credited with the first increase. This increase will be based on the interest rate of 5.25% for the first six-month period. The increase is added to the purchase price and becomes the new value of this Bond. This value is now locked in. The next increase will occur on May 1, 1996. The interest rate of 5.5% will be applied to the value of the Bond as of November 1, 1995, to create a new Bond value. This process continues for the first five years.

Each time the Bond increases in value, it then begins to earn interest at the current published short-term rate. The older short-term rates no longer impact that Bond.

Once a Bond is five years old, the interest rate applied to the Bond is the long-term market rate. Thus, as of May/2000, the long-term market rate will impact the Bond for the next six months and be credited to the Bond on November 1, 2000. After the Bond is five years old the only difference is that the long-term rate is applied to the Bond each six-month period instead of the short-term rate.

Long-Term Market Rate

The long-term market rate is determined by taking 85% of the average of the five-year Treasury yields for the six months prior to May and November. Again, don't worry, the calculations are done for you. The long-term rate is published by the Savings Bond program every May and November. The long-term rate is the only rate that will apply to a Bond after the Bond is five years old.

For the current rates, call 1-800-4USBONDS.

When Will the Interest Rates Change?

"Old Rules" (For Series E and EE Bonds purchased prior to May 1, 1995 and Savings Notes): A new individual long-term **variable rate** is published **each May and November**. This rate is averaged with the other long-term rates published for each Bond held five years or longer. The **guaranteed rate**, which was 4% at the time of writing (May 1995), last changed March 1, 1993. There is **no set time frame for any change** in the guaranteed rate.

"New Rules" (For Series EE Bonds purchased May 1, 1995, and after): The new short-term market rate and long-term market rate will be published **every May and November**. A Bond is impacted by the short-term rate if it is less than five years old. A Bond is impacted by the long-term rate if it is five years or older.

OK, maybe we have not yet harnessed Niagara Falls. Hopefully you do have a clearer sense of the interest rate issues that affect the Bonds you hold. Remember that if another illustration would be helpful, see Table 3.4, with its complete explanation at the end of this chapter.

Table 3.2   **Historic View of the Long-Term Market-Based Variable Interest Rate on U.S. Savings Bonds**

(Information Applies to the Time Period of May to October 1995)

Issue Date	Average Variable Interest Rate Over the Life of the Bond	First Variable Rate Published for Bond
through 4/30/83	7.18	11.09
5/83 to 10/83	7.02	8.64
11/83 to 4/84	6.96	9.38
5/84 to 10/84	6.85	9.95
11/84 to 4/85	6.71	10.94
5/85 to 10/85	6.51	9.49
11/85 to 4/86	6.36	8.36
5/86 to 10/86	6.26	7.02
11/86 to 4/87	6.21	6.06
5/87 to 10/87	6.22	5.84
11/87 to 4/88	6.25	7.17
5/88 to 10/88	6.18	6.90
11/88 to 4/89	6.13	7.35
5/89 to 10/89	6.04	7.81
11/89 to 4/90	5.89	6.98
5/90 to 10/90	5.79	7.01
11/90 to 4/91	5.67	7.19
5/91 to 10/91	5.50	6.57
11/91 to 4/92	5.37	6.38
5/92 to 10/92	5.23	5.58
11/92 to 4/93	5.17	5.04
5/93 to 10/93	5.19	4.78
11/93 to 4/94	5.30	4.25
5/94 to 10/94	5.64	4.70
11/94 to 4/95	6.12	5.92
5/95 to 10/95	N/A	*6.31

*This long-term rate does not impact any Bond purchased after 4/ 30/95.

Table 3.3

Guaranteed Minimum Rates through Current Maturity Period: Series E, EE, and SN

(Chart good for June 1995 only)

Issue Date	Guaranteed through Current Maturity Period
SERIES EE	
May 1995 to present	no guaranteed rate
March 1993 to April 1995	4.0
November 1986 to February 1993	6.0
July 1985 to October 1986	7.5
March 1983 to June 1985	4.0
November 1982 to February 1983	6.0
May 1981 to October 1982	6.0
November 1980 to April 1981	6.0
January 1980 to October 1980	6.0
SERIES E	
March 1978 to June 1980	4.0
December 1973 to February 1978	6.0
January 1971 to November 1973	6.0
June 1969 to December 1970	7.5
July 1968 to May 1969	7.5
March 1966 to June 1968	4.0
December 1965 to February 1966	6.0
June 1965 to November 1965	4.0
June 1959 to May 1965	6.0
December 1957 to May 1959	6.0
February 1957 to November 1957	7.5
November 1955 to January 1957	7.5
July 1955 to October 1955	4.0
May 1941 to June 1955	no longer earn interest
SAVINGS NOTES	
September 1968 to October 1970	4.0
May 1967 to August 1968	6.0

Adapted from "Guaranteed Minimum Rates for May 1995," Bureau of the Public Debt, U.S. Savings Bond Marketing Office. See Chapter 17 to order table for present month.

Table 3.4

Old Rules: Example of Computing Bond Value

Old Rules: Example of Computing Bond Value for a $1,000 Series EE Bond Purchased April 1987.

Holding Period	A — Individual Variable Rate	B — Average Variable Rate	C — Guaranteed Rate	D — Bond Value Based on Guaranteed Rate	E — Net Yield Previous 12 Month Period	F — Bond Values Based on Average Variable Rate as of Year Five...6.89%	G — Bond Values Based on Average Variable Rate as of Year Six..6.74%	H — Bond Values Based on Average Variable Rate as of Year Seven...6.48%	I — Bond Values Based on Average Variable Rate as of Year Eight...6.23%
	6.06			*Not Applicable*					
1 Year	5.84								
	7.17								
2 Years	6.90								
	7.35								
3 Years	7.81								
	6.98								
4 Years	7.01								
	7.19								
5 Years	6.57	6.89	6.00	671.96		701.56	696.49	687.78	679.50
	6.38		6.00	692.12		725.73	719.96	710.06	700.66
6 Years	5.58	6.74	6.00	712.88	6.08%	750.73	744.22	733.07	722.49
	5.04		6.00	734.27		776.59	769.31	756.82	745.00
7 Years	4.78	6.48	6.00	756.29	4.99%	803.35	795.23	781.34	768.20
	4.25		6.00	778.98		831.02	822.03	806.66	792.13
8 Years	4.70	6.23	6.00	802.35	4.54%	859.65	849.73	832.79	816.81
	5.92								

The following three pages include a complete explanation of this table.

Explanation of Table 3.4
"Old Rules": Example of Computing Bond Value

This table, and the accompanying numbers, are based on a Bond issued April 1987 with a face value of $1,000.

The example starts at the point the Bond has been held for five years (see first column titled "Holding Period"). After holding the Bond for five years two values are calculated at each semi-annual increase period. One is based on the guaranteed rate (column D) and the other is based on the average variable rate(s) (columns F through I).

Column A represents the individual market-based variable rates that have been published for this Bond. While they are announced every May and November, these rates do not impact the Bond until it has been held at least five years. At that time, the average of these rates is used to compute a value for this Bond.

Column B (Average Variable Rate) represents the average of the rates in column A. As you can see, the average of the individual market-based rates for the five-year holding period is 6.89%. At the six-year holding period, the average has dropped to 6.74%. At the seven-year holding period, the average has dropped to 6.48%. At the eight-year holding period, the average has dropped to 6.23%.

The value based on the guaranteed rate of 6% is shown in column D. At year five, the Bond value is $671.96. At year six, the Bond value is $712.88. At year seven, the Bond value is $756.29. At year eight, the Bond value is $802.35.

Now it gets interesting. Remember, at year five, two values have been calcu- lated for this Bond: the value based on the guaranteed rate ($671.96 in column D) and the value based on the average variable rate ($701.56 in column F). As a Bond owner you typically do not know that two values have been calculated. You automatically receive the higher dollar value on the government redemption tables ($701.56). And unless you follow Bonds closely, you do not know whether that value is based on the guaranteed rate or the average variable rate. Since you are following this example, however, you can see that the value is based on the average variable rate.

It is good that this Bond received a value based on the average variable rate since that value is almost $30 higher than the value the guaranteed rate would have produced. However, keep in mind that the value of your Bond is only guaranteed if you cash your Bond in the time period for which the value was published. Unlike the "New Rules," where the value of your Bond is locked in every six months, under the "Old Rules" Bond values are recalculated *every six months*, which may help or hurt the amount of increase added to a Bond depending on the specific rates involved. Examine the values and increases for this Bond at years six, seven and eight.

After holding the Bond six years, the value based on the guaranteed rate is $712.88 (column D). The value of the Bond based on the average variable rate of 6.74% is $744.22 (column G). Again the higher value is produced by the average variable rate. Take note that although the average variable rate is 6.74%, the net yield (percentage increase in value) over the last year was only 6.08% (column E). Why? The average variable rate fell from 6.89% to 6.74% during this one-year period. When taken retroactively to the date of purchase, this resulted in a net yield of 6.08%. This concept will be of particular importance as we examine years seven and eight.

At the seven-year holding period, the value of the Bond based on the guaranteed rate is $756.29 (column D). The value of the Bond based on the average variable rate of 6.48% is $781.34 (column H). Again the higher value is produced by the average variable rate. Take note that although the average variable rate is 6.48%, the net yield (percentage increase in value) for that Bond over the last year was only 4.99% (column E). Why? The average variable rate fell from 6.74% to 6.48% during this one-year period. When taken retroactively to the date of purchase, this resulted in a net yield of 4.99% for the last one-year period.

At the eight-year holding period, the value of the Bond based on the guaranteed rate is $802.35 (column D). The value of the Bond based on the average variable rate of 6.23% is $816.81 (column H). Again the higher value is produced by the average variable rate. Take note that although the average variable rate is 6.23%, the net yield (percentage increase in value) for that Bond over the last year was only 4.54% (column E). Why? The average variable rate fell from 6.48% to 6.23% during this one-year period. When taken retroactively to the date of purchase, this resulted in a net yield of 4.54% for the last one-year period.

Did the government fulfill its promise? The promise was that the Bond would receive a guaranteed rate of 6% if held for at least five years and the 6% would be the minimum rate for the Bond if the Bond is held twelve years (the original maturity period). Since the current value as of the eighth year is more than the value produced using the guaranteed rate, the promise is being kept. What about the lower net yields for current years? Note that the Savings Bond rules did not state that your minimum yield each individual year would be at least 6%, only that the cumulative yield over the holding period (five to twelve years) would be at least 6%. Since the returns in years five and six were well above the guaranteed rate, there is room for lower net yields in later years without going below the guaranteed 6% for the entire holding period.

Under what conditions can a net yield for a given year be lower than a guaranteed interest rate for a Bond? Two conditions would need to exist:

1. Previous values for a Bond would have to have been based on the average variable interest rate.
2. Recent individual variable rates would need to be lower than the previous average variable interest rate, thus pulling the average down.

Important technical caveats to this illustration: The purpose of the illustration is to explain how the interest rates work and why net yields for a given time period can be less than the guaranteed rate or variable rate in effect at that time. Additional factors that were not included in the illustration that may apply to some or all Bonds include a rounding of the average variable rate to the nearest quarter or one-hundredth percent, depending on the purchase date and/or extended maturity, and a time lag in the application of the average variable rate to a given Bond. In some cases this will cause the redemption values in the table to vary by a few pennies, from the government published redemption value.

Chapter 4

TIMING ISSUES
AND MATURITY PERIODS

▸ *Common Misconceptions*
▸ *Timing Issues at Redemption*
▸ *Timing Issues at Exchange*
▸ *Timing Issues at Final Maturity*
▸ *Timing Issues at Purchase*
▸ *What Does "Maturity" Mean?*
　—*The "Old Rules"*
　—*The "New Rules"*

If you have ever invested in stocks, you know that the timing of when to buy and when to sell is critical. Timing is also critical in real estate decisions. In fact, timing is important to virtually every financial instrument. Savings Bonds are certainly no exception.

Common Misconceptions

Once again, sorting out the truth from the fiction can help you wisely manage your Savings Bond investment.

Misconception #1: *It does not matter when you cash a Bond.*

Yes, it does. If you ignore timing issues, you can say goodbye to a maximum of up to six months of interest on most Bonds.

Misconception #2: *All Bonds increase in value at the same time.*

No. Each Bond has a unique increase date. Most Bonds increase semi-annually; however, Series EE Bonds purchased between March 1, 1993, and April 30, 1995, increase monthly up to the fifth year. Many people mistakenly think that the increase occurs every May and November because that is when the redemption tables are issued and the market-based rates are published. These two events have *no* relationship to the actual date your Bonds increase in value.

Misconception #3: *All Bonds increase in value on the issue date and six months later.*

No. This misconception is particularly damaging to owners of older Series E Bonds. Presently, there are 301 issue dates for Series E Bonds that are still earning interest. Of these dates, 60% are on Bonds that increase in value at a time *other than* the issue date (and again six months later). Nothing on the Bond tells you when the increase will occur. See Chapter 6, "Tracking Your Investment," to find out when your Bonds increases in value.

Misconception #4: *Timing is not important when exchanging for HH Bonds.*

Yes, it is. Many Bond owners exchange their Series E, EE, or Savings Notes (SN) for HH Bonds so that they can receive current income. The same timing issues that apply to the redemption of Bonds also apply to exchange. Choosing when to exchange can make a significant difference in your overall financial picture. See "Timing At Exchange" later in this chapter for more information.

Timing Issues at Redemption

Deciding when to cash a Bond rests solely with each Bond owner. The bank's role is to supply the Bond owner with the correct amount of money on the day that the Bond is redeemed. You—not the bank—are responsible for analyzing your Bond holdings and obtaining detailed advice. Unfortunately, many people do not realize the importance of timing. Here is an example from 1991 in Michigan:

A recently retired high school counselor owned U.S. Savings Bonds. He had previously cashed several $1,000 Bonds purchased in the 1950s which had not yet reached final maturity. He thought that Bonds increased in value every month and that it did not matter when they were cashed. Each of his Bonds was valued at over $5,000.

The result was that this man forfeited up to $175 on each Bond he cashed. If he cashed ten Bonds in this manner, it would mean a loss of $1,000 to $2,000 in interest. (For options on obtaining a report which provides specific information on timing issues, see Chapter 6, "Tracking Your Investment.")

A difference of even one day can mean the loss of hundreds or thousands of dollars to the Bond owner. Why? All Bonds purchased prior to March 1, 1993, or after April 30, 1995, increase in value twice a year. Cashing a Bond one day before an interest increase results in missing out on six months' interest. Seldom is the best time "accidentally" selected when Bonds are randomly redeemed.

How do I know when my Bonds Increase?

Each Bond has a unique increase date pattern. Many older Bonds increase at intervals that do not coincide with the issue date and six months later. See Chapter 6, Table 6.5, for the increase dates.

Exceptions: Any Series EE Bond purchased between March 1, 1993, and April 30, 1995, will increase in value monthly for the first five years. This change in the Bond program accompanied the drop in the guaranteed interest rate from 6% to 4%. Also, Bonds purchased prior to March 1, 1993, that are not yet thirty months old, will increase in value monthly up to the thirtieth month. (The increase will occur semi-annually thereafter.) The "new rules," effective for Series EE Bonds purchased on or after May 1, 1995, have returned the Bond program to the semi-annual increase periods. See Chapters 14 and 15 for more information.

Once the correct month is Identified, on which day should I cash my Bonds?

The increase will always occur on the first business day of the month. It will hold that value until the next scheduled increase, either the next month (for Bonds that increase monthly) or six months later (for Bonds that increase semi-annually). You will receive the same amount of money whether you redeem a Bond on the first business day of the month or the last.

Timing Issues at Exchange

An exchange occurs when you take the value of a Series E or EE Bond or SN at the time of redemption and roll it over into a HH Bond rather than accept the redemption value in cash. (This is often done to continue the tax deferral on the interest income of older Bonds and also to receive a semi-annual interest payment from the new HH Bonds.)

Suppose you have $50,000 in E Bonds that you want to exchange for HH Bonds because you want that semi-annual interest payment of 4% annually. (The author is not suggesting that this is the best alternative. See Chapter 10, "Exchanging for HH Bonds," for more considerations.)

Assume the average guaranteed interest rate on your E Bonds is 6% and that you are giving no thought to the timing of the exchange. In a typical case, you would forfeit $750 to $1,500 by not investigating the timing issue. This is money that could have purchased an additional HH Bond. If the forfeiture is $1,000, you not only missed the extra principal of an additional HH Bond, but if you had held it for ten years, that HH Bond would have netted an additional $400 in interest ($40 a year for ten years). Your loss now approaches $1,500.

See Chapter 10, "Exchanging for HH Bonds," for exchange strategies and the selective redemption alternative.

Timing Issues at Final Maturity

When a Series E or EE Bond or SN reaches final maturity (the point at which the Bond stops earning interest), it will receive the last increase on the first day of the month in which the Bond stops earning interest. For instance, a Bond purchased July 1954 will receive the last increase July 1, 1994. No additional value will be added to the Bond after that date.

Sometimes the final increase can be for a period less than six months. Bonds purchased prior to November 1965 used to have an odd number of years and months to final maturity. This has since been changed to an even forty years. For instance, a July 1956 Bond originally had a final maturity date of thirty-nine years and eight months from the date of purchase. Now this same Bond will reach final maturity in forty years—July 1996. This Bond's semi-annual increases occur every March and September. It will receive an increase in March 1996 and again in July 1996—only four months later. The final increase is the only time when the increase may not occur semi-annually.

A Series E Bond issued in 1964 will earn interest longer than a Series E Bond issued in 1966. Why?

A puzzled Bond holder wrote in reference to the Bond report she had ordered from The Savings Bond Informer:

My Bonds are Series E, purchased from 1965 to 1979. The statement gives the date that interest earnings would stop as 30 years from the date of purchase. I was under the impression that the Bonds would earn interest for 40 years. Please explain if there is an error in the statement.

The report that this Bond owner received was 100% correct. Bonds that she thought would earn interest for forty years (those purchased December 1965 and after) are only going to earn interest for thirty years.

Any E Bond that is forty years old has stopped earning interest. By the end of 1995, thirty-year old E Bonds (issued December 1965 and after) will begin to reach final maturity.

Table 4.1

Final Maturity

Series & Issue Date	Final Maturity (Total number of years Bond will earn interest)
SERIES EE	
1/80 to present	30 years
SERIES E	
12/65 to 6/80	30 years
5/41 to 11/65	40 years
SAVINGS NOTES	
5/67 to 10/70	30 years
SERIES H	
2/57 to 12/79	30 years
SERIES HH	
1/80 to present	20 years

Adapted from Final Maturity Schedule, Bureau of the Public Debt, U.S. Savings Bond Marketing Office.

Exchanging for HH Bonds at Final Maturity

Do not wait too long. Once a Bond stops earning interest, you have a one-year grace period within which to exchange it for an HH Bond. However, you will earn no interest from the date of final maturity until the exchange. If you hold the Bond for more than one year beyond final maturity, your only option is to redeem it. See Chapter 10 for information on exchanging for HH Bonds.

Timing Issues at Purchase

A Bond's issue date is the first day of the month in which it was purchased (assuming that the funds used to purchase the Bond were available to the bank the month in which it was bought). Therefore, purchasing Bonds late in the month is best because they will begin to earn interest from the first day of the month in which they were purchased.

What Does "Maturity" Mean?

The "Old Rules"

Bonds carry three different maturities: original maturity, extended maturity, and final maturity.

Original Maturity is the maximum amount of time it will take a Bond to reach face value at the guaranteed interest rate. This date is set at purchase, regardless of when the Bond actually reaches face value.

For example, an EE Bond purchased in 1994 has an original maturity period of eighteen years. The guaranteed interest rate is 4%. If this Bond ends up with an average market-based interest rate of 5%, it will reach face value in about fourteen years. However, the original maturity period will still be eighteen years. This means that the guaranteed rate of 4% will not change until the Bond enters an extended maturity at the end of the eighteenth year.

Extended Maturity periods are always ten years long, except for the last one, which can be less. An extended maturity period begins when your Bond reaches the end of the original maturity period. Bonds issued prior to May 1, 1995, will take on a new guaranteed rate as they enter their extended maturity period. A Bond may have more than one extended maturity period. See Table 4.2 for clarification.

Final Maturity is the date after which the Bond will no longer earn interest.

Why is this knowledge critical? Bond owners have sometimes been counseled to redeem Bonds when they reach "maturity." Maturity has been incorrectly defined as "reaching face value." The result is that the Bond owners cash Bonds that would have continued to earn interest for another ten or twenty years. The Bond owner also has to declare the full amount of interest in the year of redemption. It really hurts when this happens to people who are only a few years from retirement: They are declaring the interest income when they are most likely in the highest tax bracket of their lives.

Review an example of how the term "maturity," as described above, would work on an EE Bond purchased in November 1986. See Table 4.2, the third line under Series EE.

A Bond purchased in November 1986 will earn interest for thirty years. At the guaranteed rate of 6%, the Bond will reach face value in twelve years. (Note: If this Bond earns more than 6%, it will reach face value in less than twelve years. The original maturity period, however, is still twelve years.) At the end of twelve years, the Bond will enter a ten-year extended maturity period. At the end of this extended maturity period, the Bond will be twenty-two years old. Since a Bond purchased in November 1986 earns interest for thirty years, the final maturity period will only be eight years.

Table 4.2 provides the original maturity periods and extension periods for Series E and EE Bonds and SNs.

Why All Bonds Are Not the Same

The original maturity period of a Bond can range anywhere from four years, six months to eighteen years. The variance is a result of different interest rates and purchase prices at the time of issue. As previously stated, some Bonds earn interest for thirty years and others, for forty years. In Table 4.2, note that a Bond with an original maturity period of eight years, eleven months (purchased May 1959) will have a maturity schedule of three ten-year extensions and a final extension of one year, one month.

Each time a Bond enters an extended maturity period, the guaranteed interest rate for that Bond becomes whatever the current guaranteed rate is at that time. A Bond purchased in January 1984 had an original maturity period of ten years and a guaranteed rate of 7.5%. Since the guaranteed rate was 4% on January 1, 1994, this Bond now has a guaranteed rate of 4% for the next ten years.

Remember: The average market-based variable rate can be a factor on any Bond five years or older. See Chapter 3, "Understanding Interest Rates."

The "New Rules"

The Savings Bond program threw an interesting twist into the new rules. A Bond will receive a one-time catch-up increase in value to face value if the Bond has not yet reached face value by year seventeen. In essence that guarantees a minimum rate of about 4.12% if you hold the Bond for seventeen years. Hmm...Sounds like a guarantee to me.

The original maturity period for Bonds issued under the new rules is seventeen years. These Bonds will continue to earn interest for a full thirty years from the issue date.

What rate of interest will be earned after original maturity? The Treasury Department has not committed itself to a specific interest rate structure or pattern beyond seventeen years at the time of writing. While none of the Bonds issued under the new rules will reach the seventeen-year mark until 2012, this will be an important issue for Bond owners to watch.

Author's Note: The original maturity period for Bonds under the new rules is significant in the unlikely event that the seventeen-year catchup is necessary. It is also significant because the Treasury could assign different interest rates and/or interest rate structures to your Bonds as they enter extended maturity periods. It would make sense for a Bond to continue to earn interest at the long-term market rate for each six-month period as it enters an extended maturity period, but that is not a sure thing. The final maturity period is important as always, because the Bond will not earn any more interest after that date. See Chapter 15 for more details on the "New Rules."

Take time to learn about your Savings Bond investment. The number of people who relate stories of misinformation and financial mishap to The Savings Bond Informer, Inc. are evidence enough: Knowing each stage your Bonds will go through is critical in avoiding costly mistakes. One of the most common questions Bond owners make is "I know my Bonds are mature, what do I do now?" After reading this chapter, hopefully you now understand what "maturity" means and why timing issues play an important role in maximizing your Savings Bond investment.

Table 4.2

Guide to Extended and Final Maturity Periods

Issue Date	Original Maturity Period	First Extended Maturity Period	Additional Extended Period	Additional Extended Period	Additional Extended Period	Final Maturity (total number of years Bond will earn interest)
SERIES EE						
5/95 to present	17 years	10 years	3 years			30 years
3/93 to 4/95	18 years	10 years	2 years			30 years
11/86 to 2/93	12 years	10 years	8 years			30 years
11/82 to 10/86	10 years	10 years	10 years			30 years
5/81 to 10/82	8 years	10 years	10 years	2 years		30 years
11/80 to 4/81	9 years	10 years	10 years	1 year		30 years
1/80 to 10/80	11 years	10 years	9 years			30 years
SERIES E						
12/73 to 6/80	5 years	10 years	10 years	5 years		30 years
6/69 to 11/73	5 years, 10 months	10 years	10 years	4 years, 2 months		30 years
12/65 to 5/69	7 years	10 years	10 years	3 years		30 years
6/59 to 11/65	7 years, 9 months	10 years	10 years	10 years	2 years, 3 months	40 years
2/57 to 5/59	8 years, 11 months	10 years	10 years	10 years	1 year, 1 months	40 years
5/55 to 1/57	9 years, 8 months	10 years	10 years	10 years	4 months	40 years
All Series E Bonds over 40 years old have stopped earning interest.						
SAVINGS NOTES						
5/67 to 10/70	4 years, 6 months	10 years	10 years	5 years, 6 months		30 years

ORGANIZING YOUR BONDS

- ▸ *The Importance of Organizing Your Bonds*
- ▸ *What Information Is Needed for Record Keeping?*
- ▸ *Where Should Bonds Be Kept?*
- ▸ *How Should Bonds Be Organized?*
- ▸ *Where Should Your Bond Record Be Kept?*
- ▸ *"To Do" List*

You may be a very organized person. The books on your shelves may be in alphabetical order by the author's last name; all your spices may be lined up by name, container size, and country of origin. On the other hand, there are those of us who have trouble matching our socks each morning. As for organization—please!

Whatever your personal style, remember that Bonds are the "do-it-yourself" investment. Record keeping is your responsibility.

The Importance of Organizing Your Bonds

When it comes to U.S. Savings Bonds, organization is a good idea. Why? Americans are currently holding almost $2 billion in Savings Bonds that have stopped earning interest. Many of these Bonds are tucked in dresser drawers, stuffed in shoe boxes, or locked in safe-deposit boxes. In addition, many Bonds remain unclaimed because deceased Bond owners kept no records for their heirs.

Most people treat their assets with considerable attention and scrutiny. Your Savings Bond investment should be no different. If a salesman tried to sell you a financial investment with the closing pitch, "Don't pay any attention to this for the next twenty to thirty years," you would probably tell him to get lost. Yet, this is how many people handle their Savings Bonds.

The ability to provide detailed information to the Bureau of the Public Debt (BPD)—should the Bonds ever become lost, stolen, or ruined—is a great reason to keep good records. True, the BPD does keep a master file on all Bonds issued, but it can take up to a month or more to obtain records from them. The more information you can provide, the quicker they can research and replace Bonds for legitimate claims.

What Information Is Needed for Record Keeping?

The following information should be recorded for each Bond that you own:

✓ Serial Number (including Series E, EE, H, HH, or SN)
✓ Registration (names on Bond, S.S.#, address)
✓ Date of Issue (top right-hand corner)
✓ Face value (or denomination)

Table 5.1 can be used to record this information. (See Chapter 6, "Tracking Your Investment," before you start. If you decide to fill in all the details for your Bond, you may prefer to use the Do-It-Yourself Worksheet.)

Photocopies as Backup Records

If you do not feel like writing down all that information, make photocopies of your Bonds. The front of the Bond has all of the important information, so you don't need to copy the back. According to the Bond consultants at the BPD, photocopying and faxing copies of Bonds is legal. Photocopies can in no way be negotiated nor do they have any monetary value. But they can serve as a valuable resource to reconstruct Bond holdings that have perished or become lost or been stolen.

Where Should Bonds Be Kept?

While U.S. Savings Bonds do not need ultra-expensive housing, do not be careless. You might want to do better than one Bond owner who returned fragments of what appeared to be a Savings Bond to the Federal Reserve Bank. It seems the color of the Bond resembled the color of the dog's food. Fido had a tasty little snack, leaving only bits of a president's face.

If peace of mind comes best to you through a safe-deposit box, keep your Bonds there. This may make sense if you want to restrict a co-owner's access to the Bonds. (See Chapter 12 for additional information on the rights of co-owners.)

Safe-deposit boxes generally cost between $20 and $200, depending on the box size and the part of the country you live in. If you only have a few Bonds, the safe-deposit box's rental may cost more than the interest you earn.

If you choose to keep the Bonds at home, keep them together in an organized fashion. If they are spread out in books, drawers, under the bed, and sewn into jacket liners, your heirs may never find them. Leave directions with your will outlining where the Bonds are kept.

How Should Bonds Be Organized?

There is no exact rule on how Bonds should be organized. Certain guidelines, however, will make life easier for you and anyone else who has to deal with your Bonds (such as the Federal Reserve Bank, if your Bonds have to be retitled). Several different patterns of organization are possible, the worst being the "fifty-two card pick-up" method, which confuses everyone.

One way to sort Bonds is by series. There are five common series of Bonds: E, EE, H, HH, or SN (Savings Notes or Freedom Shares).

Within each series, Bonds can be further sorted by issue date (top right-hand corner), face value, or registration.

Where Should Your Bond Record Be Kept?

Keep one copy of your records with your Bonds. An identical copy should be kept in a place safe from fire and theft. This second copy is very important. If the Bonds are lost, stolen, or destroyed, the record will make the replacement process much easier.

"To Do" List

✓ Organize Bonds by series, then by issue date, face value, or registration.

✓ Use Bond record grid to note serial number, registration, issue date, and face value for each Bond.

✓ Make a photocopy of the completed Bond record.

✓ Put one copy of the Bond record with the Bonds; the other in a different spot.

✓ Store the Bonds in a safe place.

✓ Keep Bond information with your will, stating location of the Bonds and Bond records.

Table 5.1.

A Record of United States Savings Bonds
Name(s), address, and Social Security number on Bonds:

_____

_____

_____

Issue Date (Month/Year)	Face Value	Serial Number	Issue Date (Month/Year)	Face Value	Serial Number

40

Chapter 6

TRACKING YOUR INVESTMENT

> ▸ *Options for Tracking Your Investment*
> ▸ *The Most Important Information to Know about Your Bonds*
> ▸ *How to Build a Savings Bond Statement*
> ▸ *Understanding Your Savings Bond Statement*

Managing money has become an increasingly hot topic in the 1990s. Yet, tracking your Savings Bond investment may be a new concept to you. Treat your U.S. Savings Bonds as you would any investment.

Options For Tracking
Your Investment

To determine the interest rates, timing issues, values, and maturity dates for each Bond you own, you will need a little knowledge, a few resources, and some time. There are basically two options.

Option #1: Use the *Do-it-Yourself Worksheet* (Table 6.1) and follow the steps in this chapter to complete a statement of your Savings Bond holdings. The costs include a phone call or letter to request the current government tables and the time to select and compute the information that applies to your Bonds.

Option #2: Contact The Savings Bond Informer, Inc. (TSBI) to do the research for you. You will need to send a list of your Bonds (month/year of purchase, face value, and series) or a photocopy of all Bonds and they will produce a report that, in the words of *Newsweek* (October 4, 1993), is "... easy-to-read, easy-to-understand." An example of a TSBI report is shown in Figures 6.1 and 6.2. The cost for the service depends on the number of Bonds to be analyzed, starting at $12. A complete price list is given in the resource section (Chapter 17) and an order form has been included at the back of the book. Each Bond analysis addresses all of the primary questions outlined below.

The remainder of this chapter is designed to help Bond owners who prefer to do their own research and track their own investments. If you like working with numbers, this can be both challenging and fun.

Following are the important questions that must be answered about each Bond you own.

The Most Important Information
to Know about Your Bonds

Detailed Questions:

1. What are my Bonds worth now?
2. How much interest has accrued to date?
3. When will my Bonds reach final maturity?
4. When do my Bonds increase in value?
5. What is the guaranteed interest rate on my Bonds?
6. What is the average variable interest rate on my Bonds?
7. When will my Bonds enter extended maturity periods?

Summary Questions:

8. What is the total value of my Bond investment?
9. How much did I pay for my Bonds?
10. What is the total interest earned on my Bonds?
11. When will my Bonds reach face value?

An answer to each question is critical for wise management of your Bond investment. The following is a brief explanation of why each answer is important.

1. **What are my Bonds worth now?** *Your Bond holdings may be worth as little as half of their face value or as much as six times their face value.* Knowing the exact value of each Bond will provide you with an accurate assessment of this vehicle within your investment portfolio. Practically speaking, if you want to cash some Bonds next month, knowing the values will help determine how many you need to cash.

2. **How much interest has accrued to date?** For most Bond owners, interest becomes a tax liability in the year the Bond is cashed or reaches final maturity (exceptions may include Bond owners who report interest annually, Bonds that are eligible for the tax-free feature, and Bonds exchanged for HH upon final maturity). For tax-planning purposes, it is important to know how much interest you have accrued. (See Chapter 8 for more on tax issues.)

3. **When will my Bonds reach final maturity?** Plan ahead. Remember that *Americans are holding almost $2 billion of Bonds that have stopped earning interest.* Do not join that crowd. Make sure you know when each of your Bonds will stop earning interest and have a plan for redemption or exchange. Chapters 10 and 13 will help you do this.

4. **When do my Bonds increase in value?** Would you want to give away five months of interest on each investment you have? If you do not know the timing issues on your Bonds, you will unknowingly end up making another contribution to Uncle Sam. Each Bond issued before March 1993 (and that is at least thirty months old) or after April 1995 will increase in value twice a year. *Cash a Bond one day before an increase and you will forfeit six months of interest.* For Bonds purchased prior to December 1973, the increases do not always fall on the issue date and six months later. You will need a table to help you determine the correct dates.

5. **What is the guaranteed interest rate on my Bonds?** As was discussed in Chapter 3, each Bond purchased prior to May 1, 1995 has a unique guaranteed and average variable interest rate. Knowing these rates will help you determine whether to sell or hold.

6. **What is the market-based variable interest rate on my Bonds?** Since Bonds do have a market-based rate, tracking the variable rate will help you determine the direction the average variable rate is going for Bonds purchased prior to May 1, 1995. For Bonds purchased after April 30, 1995, a specific short- or long-term variable rate will be assigned to your Bond.

7. **When will my Bonds enter extended maturity periods?** Bonds purchased prior to May 1, 1995 assume a new guaranteed interest rate when they enter an extended maturity period. Bonds that were earning 7.5% may drop to a guaranteed rate of 4%. You need to know which Bonds are affected when. The details on maturity and extended maturity periods are presented in Chapter 4.

8. **What is the total value of my Bond investment?** If you are looking at a large purchase, your Bonds might provide just the money you need, so it is important to know exactly how much they are worth. This will also give you an accurate number to put into your net worth statement.

9. **How much did I pay for my Bonds?** This is your original cost, what you actually paid for the Bonds (it is the cost basis even if you received the Bonds as a gift). Face values can be misleading. Remember the advertisements on TV, "Buy this or that and get a free $200 U.S. Savings Bond." That $200 EE Bond was bought for $100.

10. **What is the total interest earned on my Bonds?** If you cash all of your Bonds at one time, this is the amount you would have to report as interest income. Your tax bracket would then determine how much you pay in taxes.

11. **When will my Bonds reach face value?** Five years? Seven? Ten? Twelve? Eighteen? Any of those answers could be correct depending on when your Bond was purchased. The length of time depends on the purchase price and the interest rates assigned to a particular Bond. The most important issue related to this question is the date that your Bond reaches the end of the original maturity period (at which point the Bond will be worth at least face value). At that time it enters an extended maturity period. For Bonds purchased prior to May 1, 1995, entering an extended maturity period results in a new guaranteed rate being assigned to the Bond.

How to Build a Savings Bond Statement

Resources

In order to build a Bond statement, you will need several tables. The first two are a *Do-It-Yourself Worksheet* (Table 6.1) and a *Summary*

Statement (Table 6.2). In addition, you will need to send for the following government tables which have been reproduced at the end of this chapter for illustrative purposes only:

- ✓Guaranteed Minimum Rates and Original Maturity Periods (see sample, Table 6.3)
- ✓ Semi-annual Interest Rate Bulletin (see sample, Table 6.4)
- ✓ Interest Accrual Dates (Tables 6.5 and 6.6)
- ✓Table of Redemption Values for Series E and EE Bonds and SN (see sample, Table 6.7)

Important: All of the above tables except Tables 6.5 and 6.6 will change over time, so the ones printed in this book will soon be outdated. (Note: Only a portion of the Tables of Redemption Values has been reprinted.) **For this reason, use these tables only for the practice exercises in this chapter. Before you calculate the information for your Bonds, obtain the most recent versions. They may be ordered from the Bureau of the Public Debt or your regional Federal Reserve Bank. See Chapter 17 for addresses and phone numbers.**

Once you have gathered the above aids, you will need a pencil, calculator, scratch pad, and soft drink—and you are ready to begin. That is, assuming you have already organized your Bonds. If not, it would be advisable to quickly review and follow the directions as outlined in Chapter 5, "Organizing Your Bonds."

Instructions for the Do-It-Yourself Worksheet

Friendly hint: You may find it helpful to read the entire set of instructions that follow, Steps 1 through 10, before you begin to enter information from your Bonds onto your worksheets. This will save you from numerous u#n@p!r*I#n@t*a%b#l@e outbursts and give you a general sense of direction. In addition, you may decide that you only want to calculate the value and maturity dates and so choose to skip some of the steps. *The following instructions only apply to Series E, EE, and Savings Notes, not to H and HH Bonds.* (See Chapter 10 for information on H and HH Bonds).

STEP 1: Locate the *Do-It-Yourself Worksheet*, Table 6.1, at the end of this chapter and complete the information above the table (i.e., "This information is being calculated as of..."; this is the month you will refer to when you get to Step 5). Next, fill in the first three columns of the worksheet with information taken from your Bonds. The Bond pictured in Figure 6.3 and the first line of the worksheet will serve as an example.

Figure 6.3   **Series EE Savings Bond**

Column A: Series. The series identification is listed on the front of the Bond, usually in an upper corner. You will record either E, EE, or SN in column A. (It does get more exciting, really.)

Column B: Date of Purchase Month/Year. The issue date can be found in the top right-hand corner of your Bond, just below the series identification. (Ignore the issue stamp that is below the issue date.) The issue date will determine which set of information applies to your Bond. Record this in column B.

Column C: Face Value of Bond. The face value of the Bond is the amount printed on the Bond in the upper left-hand corner. The face value of the Bond is *not* the purchase price. List this in column C.

> **Summary**: The Series EE Bond pictured above has an issue date of September 1986 and a face value of $75. This has already been recorded in columns A, B, and C of your worksheet. (Older Bonds may not have the series and face value in the same place as that of the EE Bond previously pictured. That information will, however, appear somewhere on the front of the Bond.)

STEP 2: Locate the *Guaranteed Minimum Rates Table*, Table 6.3. The table at the end of this chapter is included as a reference for practice purposes.

On your *Do-It-Yourself Worksheet*, you have listed a month and year of purchase (the issue date) of each Bond in column B. Note: If your issue date is May/1995 or after, list N/A (not applicable) for that Bond in column D and skip to Step 3. Using this issue date, go to the left-hand column of the Guaranteed Minimum Rate Sheet, under the section for your series, and find the range of dates within which your Bond was purchased. Using that line look across the table to the third column under the heading of "Guaranteed Through Current Maturity Period." This is the guaranteed rate that currently applies to your Bond: Insert this number in column D.

> **Summary**: From Table 6.3, we can see that the September 1986 Bond has a current guaranteed rate of 7.5%. This is recorded in column D of your worksheet.

STEP 3: Locate the *Semi-annual Interest Rate Bulletin*, Table 6.4. Again using the month and year of purchase, locate the range of dates within which your Bond's issue date would fall. Once you have located the range of dates for your Bond, move across the page to the far right to the column under the heading "Average Market-Based Rate." This number is the average of the variable rates published for your Bond to date. Write this number in column E of your report.

> **Summary**: The Bond from September 1986 has an average variable interest rate of 6.27%. This is recorded in column E of the example line on your worksheet.

Special Note for Step 3: If you have Bonds that were purchased after April 30, 1995, the variable rate assigned to your Bond in the Semi-annual Interest Rate Bulletin is not averaged with any other published rates. That rate alone will apply to your Bond for the next six-month period.

STEP 4: Locate the *Interest Accrual Dates Tables*, Tables 6.5 and 6.6. Using the month and year of purchase, locate the interest accrual date within the box that accommodates your issue date. Then, match the month that your Bond was purchased to month in the left column of the box. The two months listed to the right of your month are the months in which your Bond will increase in value. List these two months in column F on your worksheet.

> **Summary**: On the interest accrual table, the increase dates listed for the September 1986 Bond are September and March. This is recorded in column F of your worksheet.

STEP 5: Now it is time to calculate the redemption value for your Bonds. For Steps 5 and 6 you will use the *Table of Redemption Values*, Table 6.7. This is the most basic redemption value table. This table has been chosen for two reasons: First, it is the most common table available; second, it is free. (The government does publish a more extensive table that does not require any calculations; the cost is $5.

See Chapter 17 under the subtitle "Tables for Analyzing Bonds On Your Own" for ordering information.)

Locate the year your Bond was purchased (in the left-hand column). Note that spot and look at the top of the table. There are six consecutive months listed (with year). Find the column that gives the date in which you wish to value your Bonds: This is the date you wrote above the table on the *Do-It-Yourself Worksheet*. Staying within the corresponding year that the Bond was purchased, go down the column and find the month that your Bond was issued (there may be a range of months without listing your specific month; if that is the case, find the range for your Bond). Note the point where these two come together (intersect, collide, converge, join—you get the picture).

The value listed to the right of this point is the value of the smallest denomination for that particular series. The value you have located is the value of a $50 Series EE Bond or a $25 Series E Bond or SN. **If you are valuing Bonds other than a $50 EE or a $25 E, some calculations will be necessary to arrive at the correct value.**

If you have a Series E Bond and the face value is other than $25, divide the face value of your Bond by 25. Multiply that number by the value you identified in the redemption table. Copy the result into column G on your worksheet.

If you have a Series EE Bond and the face value is other than $50, divide the face value by 50. Multiply that number by the value you identified in the redemption table. Copy the result into column G on your worksheet.

> **Summary**: For our September 1986 Bond, locate 1986 in the Issue Date column (the first column on the left). Note that spot and then find the "calculated as of" date which, in this case, is August 1994. As you move across the top of the page, you will see that August 1994 is the fourth column of data. Go down that column to the point where the column and row intersect. You see the following months listed:
>
> | | |
> |---|---|
> | Nov.-Dec. | 39.68 |
> | Sep.-Oct. | 43.44 |
> | Mar.-Aug. | 45.06 |
> | Jan.-Feb. | 46.76 |
>
> Since your Bond was issued in September 1986, you want the range of "Sep.-Oct." The value of a $50 EE Bond issued September 1986 is $43.44, as of August 1994. However, the example Bond has a $75 face value. Using the instructions above, the EE Bond is divided by 50. The result is 1.5. Now multiply the $43.44 by 1.5. The result

is the value you see listed in column G on the example line, $65.16.

STEP 6: Once you have determined the value of your Bonds, you can calculate the interest. The basic formula is this:

Current Value - Purchase Price = Interest Accrued

The current value has been written in column G as a result of Step 5. The purchase price is different for each series, so make sure you use the number that applies to your series:

Series EE: Purchase price is 50% of face value;
Series E: Purchase price is 75% of face value;
Savings Notes: Purchase price is 81% of face value.

The face value has been recorded in column C of your statement. Once you have calculated the interest accumulated, list it in column H.

> **Summary**: The current value of the Bond in the example is $65.16. Since this is an EE Bond with a face value of $75, the purchase price was $75 x 50% = $37.50. Using the formula noted above, one can conclude:

Current Value ($65.16) - Purchase Price ($37.50) = Interest Accumulated ($27.66)

STEP 7: If your Bond was purchased in November 1965 or before, add forty years to the issue date to determine the final maturity date. If your Bond was purchased in December 1965 or after, add thirty years to the issue date to determine the final maturity date. List the results of your calculations in column I for each Bond.

> **Summary**: The September 1986 Bond will reach final maturity in thirty years; therefore, the final maturity date is September 2016. List this in column I.

Optional Step: The last column on the *Do-it-Yourself Worksheet* has space for the serial number to be listed. Putting your serial number is not critical to determining any of the interest rates, values, or timing issues. However, if you do not have your serial numbers recorded on any other documents, this column will provide a useful place to record that information.

Instructions for the Summary Statement

The summary information will be written in on the *Summary Statement*, Table 6.2. This page will reflect the total redemption value of your Bonds, the total interest accumulated, and the total purchase price.

STEP 8: To determine the total redemption value of your Bonds, add all of the numbers in column G of your worksheet. Note this on the summary sheet.

STEP 9: For the total interest accumulated on your Bonds to date, add all of the numbers in column H of your worksheet. Record the total on the summary sheet.

STEP 10: If your calculations are correct, the difference between the totals you calculated in Steps 8 and 9 will be the total purchase price of all of your Bonds. Subtract the total interest accumulated on your Bonds from the total redemption value. Write this total on your summary page for "Total Purchase Price."

Want to double check? All E Bonds were purchased for 75% of face value, EE Bonds are purchased for 50% of face value, and Savings Notes were purchased for 81% of face value.

Congratulations. You have finished! (Or you cheated and skipped to this line!)

If you loved it, then the author recommends repeating this process every one to two years. The only columns of your report that will remain the same are columns F and I. Columns D, E, G, and H will change over time.

If you hated it, or quit, do not despair. Get a list of your Bonds together (or photocopy the Bonds) and send them to The Savings Bond Informer, Inc. As mentioned, they will perform the calculations for a small fee.

Understanding Your Savings
Bond Statement

The following is a brief explanation of the information that you have listed in each column. **Disclaimer**: *This explanation does not assure that the calculations you performed are accurate.*

Column

A = Series identification

B = The month and year in which you purchased your Savings Bond

C = The face value of the Bond, the dollar amount printed on the front of the Bond (A Bond may be worth more or less than its face value. The current worth of your Bond is given in column G.)

D = This is the guaranteed interest rate, published by the government, for your Bond in the *current maturity period.* For Bonds purchased prior to March 1, 1993, you must hold your Bond at least five years from the date of purchase to be eligible for the guaranteed rate of interest listed in this column. **If your Bond is less than five years old, read the interest rate rules that apply to your Bond later in this chapter.** It is possible to receive an interest rate higher than the guaranteed rate. There is no guaranteed rate for Series EE Bonds purchased after April 30, 1995.

E = This is your current average variable interest rate for Bonds purchased prior to May 1, 1995. This rate is only significant in its relationship to other variable rates published over the life of your Bond. **To be eligible for the average variable rate you must hold your Bond at least five years.** A variable rate has been published every six months since November 1982. If your Bond is five years old or older, then all the individual variable rates published during the life of your Bond are averaged. If the average of the variable rates produces a greater redemption value than the guaranteed rates in effect over the life of your Bond, then you automatically receive the rate(s) that produces the highest redemption value. For Bonds purchased prior to 1988, the average variable rates have been declining because the recently published individual variable rates are pulling the average down. The average variable rate is rounded up or down to the nearest one-hundredth or one-quarter percent. If the Bond was purchased May 1989 or after, or if the Bond entered into an extended maturity period in May 1989 or after, then the rate is rounded to the nearest one-hundredth percent. Otherwise the rate will be rounded to the nearest one-quarter percent.

"New Rules": If your Bond was purchased after April 30, 1995, there is no averaging of the market-based rates. The individual rate that is published is the rate that your Bond will earn for the next six-month period. A new rate is assigned to these Bonds every six months. If your Bond is less than five years old, than the short-term variable rate will apply to your Bond. If your Bond is five years old or older, then the long-term variable rate will apply to your Bond.

F = Interest is added to your Bond on the first business day of the two months listed in this column. If you are planning to redeem or exchange Bonds, remember that the value of your Bond increases only twice a year: on the first business day of the month listed for that Bond and again six months later. (This may or may not be the same month as your issue date.) If your Bond is less than thirty months old or if your Bond was purchased after March 1993, read the new rate information on the following page.

G = This is the redemption value of your Bond as of the date listed below your name.

H = This is the interest income that you have earned on your Bond. If you redeem a Bond, the bank reports this to the IRS as interest income.

I = The month and year listed in this column represent the last time this Bond will increase in value. Continuing to hold the Bond after the first business day of the month listed will result in no additional interest.

Summary Statement Explanation

Total redemption value is the total value of all the Bonds listed on your worksheet as of the date on your statement.

Total interest accumulated on Bonds is the total interest accumulated on all the Bonds in your worksheet(s). If you were to redeem all the Bonds in your statement, the bank that redeemed the Bonds would report this amount to the IRS on a 1099-INT.

Total purchase price is the amount that was actually paid for the Bonds listed in your statement.

Important Information for Bonds Less than Five Years Old and Purchased Prior to March 1, 1993

The following information applies to Bonds purchased between November 1, 1986, and February 28, 1993. You must hold these Bonds at least five years to be eligible for the average variable interest rate listed in column E on your statement. If you redeem a Bond that is less than five years old, you will receive a fixed rate of interest that is less than your guaranteed rate (column D). This guaranteed interest rate starts at 4.16% in year one and increases approximately 0.5% a year to 6% in year five. Once you have held the Bond five years, the government will apply the rate that will produce the greatest redemption value (guaranteed or variable) to calculate your redemption value. Bonds purchased between November 1986 and February 1993 and held for at least five years are guaranteed a minimum interest rate of 6% (through the original maturity period, which is twelve years).

All Bonds purchased between November 1986 and February 1993 are guaranteed to reach face value in twelve years or less. If the average variable rate is greater than 6% over the first twelve years of a Bond, it can reach face value in less than twelve years. These Bonds will realize their first increase at six months and will increase monthly until they are thirty months old. After that, the increase will occur semi-annually until the Bond stops earning interest.

Rate Information for Bonds Purchased March 1993 to April 1995

All EE Bonds purchased between March 1, 1993, to April 30, 1995, will carry a guaranteed interest rate of 4% for the original maturity period. EE Bonds purchased during this time period will increase in value monthly until they are five years old. If, at that point, the average variable rate is greater than 4% (which it likely will be, since none of the individual rates has been lower than 4.25% for the history of the variable rate program), then the increase will convert to a semi-annual increase schedule. All new Bonds must be held at least six months.

New Rate Information for Bonds Purchased After April 30, 1995

The new rules will be easier to understand and follow. At any given point in time, only one interest rate will apply to a Bond. (Under the old system, a guaranteed rate and a blend of variable rates are assigned to each Bond). If the Bond is less than five years old, a short-term variable rate will be assigned to a Bond every six months. If the Bond is held five years or longer, a long-term variable rate is assigned to the Bond every six months. Under this system, what you see is what you get. There is no guaranteed rate under the new rules. There is no retroactive feature attached to any of the market-based rates.

As you can see, tracking your Bond investment provides information essential to understanding and managing your Bonds. You can now make decisions based on facts and knowledge rather than opinion and hearsay.

Figure 6.1
Sample of The Savings Bond Informer, Inc. Savings Bond Detail Listing

TSBI: 0010737B

Page 1

Detail Listing of Savings Bonds for:

NAME OF BOND OWNER

As of March 1994

The Savings Bond Informer, Inc.
P.O. Box 9249
Detroit, MI 48209
(313) 843-1910

A	B	C	D	E	F	G	H	I
Bond Number & Series	Date of Purchase Month/Year	Face Value of Bond	Guaranteed Interest Rate in Current Maturity Period	Current Average Variable Interest Rate	Months that Bond Increases in Value	Redemption Value as of Statement Date	Interest Accumulated on Bond to Date	Bond will stop earning interest after...
1-E	JAN/1956	$25	7.50	7.38	SEP & MAR	$165.06	$146.31	JAN/1996
2-E	SEP/1959	$100	6.00	7.38	JUN & DEC	$559.08	$484.08	SEP/1999
3-E	MAR/1963	$1,000	6.00	7.38	DEC & JUN	$5,281.20	$4,531.20	MAR/2003
4-E	FEB/1966	$500	6.00	7.38	FEB & AUG	$2,277.00	$1,902.00	FEB/1996
5-E	JUL/1971	$75	6.00	7.38	MAY & NOV	$256.74	$200.49	JUL/2001
6-EE	DEC/1980	$200	6.00	7.38	DEC & JUN	$278.40	$178.40	DEC/2010
7-EE	FEB/1984	$5,000	4.00	7.15	FEB & AUG	$5,222.00	$2,722.00	FEB/2014
8-EE	FEB/1986	$50	7.50	6.49	FEB & AUG	$45.06	$20.06	FEB/2016
9-EE	MAY/1988	$10,000	6.00	6.32	MAY & NOV	$7,112.00	$2,112.00	MAY/2018
10-EE	AUG/1993	$100	4.00	4.52	MONTHLY	$51.20	$1.20	AUG/2023
					Page Totals:	$21,247.74	$12,297.74	

63

Figure 6.2

Sample of The Savings Bond Informer, Inc. Savings Bond Summary Report

** IMPORTANT **

THE SAVINGS BOND INFORMER, INC. PRESENTS...
A STATEMENT OF THE SAVINGS BONDS HELD BY:

NAME OF BOND OWNER

As of March 1994

10 Bonds in this statement

Purchase Price: $8,950.00

Total interest accumulated on bonds: $12,297.74
(total of column H)

Total redemption value of bonds: $21,247.74
(total of column G)

Do-It-Yourself Worksheet

Table 6.1

This information is being calculated as of: _____ (month/year)

Name of Bond Owner: _____

Page # _____

A Series	B Date of Purchase Month/ Year (Issue Date)	C Face Value of Bond	D Guaranteed Interest Rate in Current Maturity Period	E Variable Interest Rate: Average or Individual	F Months that Bond Increases in Value	G Redemption Value as of Date Listed Above	H Interest Accumulated on Bond to Date	I Date that Bond Will Stop Earning Interest	Optional Column Serial Number
EE	Sep/86	$75	7.5	6.27	Sep & Mar	65.16	27.66	Sep/2016	

Table 6.2

A DO-IT-YOURSELF SUMMARY STATEMENT
OF SAVINGS BONDS HELD BY:

As of _____

Total redemption value on Bonds listed on worksheets:
(total of column G) $ _____

Total interest accumulated on Bonds listed on worksheets:
(total of column H) $ _____

Total purchase price: $ _____

Table 6.3

Guaranteed Minimum Rates
and Original Maturity Periods

For Series EE, E and Savings Notes (Chart good for practice only-Information as of August 1994)

Issue Date	Original Maturity Period	Guaranteed Through Current Maturity Period	Life of Bond (years)
SERIES EE			
March 1993 to August 1994	18 yrs.	4.0	30
November 1986 to February 1993	12 yrs.	6.0	30
September 1984 to October 1986	10 yrs.	7.5	30
March 1983 to August 1984	10 yrs.	4.0	30
November 1982 to February 1983	10 yrs.	6.0	30
May 1981 to October 1982	8 yrs.	6.0	30
November 1980 to April 1981	9 yrs.	6.0	30
January 1980 to October 1980	11 yrs.	6.0	30
SERIES E			
September 1979 to June 1980	5 yrs.	7.5	30
March 1978 to August 1979	5 yrs.	4.0	30
December 1973 to February 1978	5 yrs.	6.0	30
January 1971 to November 1973	5 yrs. 10 mos.	6.0	30
June 1969 to December 1970	5 yrs. 10 mos.	7.5	30
September 1967 to May 1969	7 yrs.	7.5	30
March 1966 to August 1967	7 yrs.	4.0	30
December 1965 to February 1966	7 yrs.	6.0	30
June 1965 to November 1965	7 yrs. 9 mos.	4.0	40
June 1959 to May 1965	7 yrs. 9 mos.	6.0	40
December 1957 to May 1959	8 yrs. 11 mos.	6.0	40
February 1957 to November 1957	8 yrs. 11 mos.	7.5	40
January 1955 to January 1957	9 yrs. 8 mos.	7.5	40
September 1954 to December 1954	9 yrs. 8 mos.	4.0	40
May 1941 to August 1954		no longer earn interest	40
SAVINGS NOTES			
March 1970 to October 1970	4 yrs. 6 mos.	7.5	30
September 1968 to February 1970	4 yrs. 6 mos.	4.0	30
May 1967 to August 1968	4 yrs. 6 mos.	6.0	30

Adapted from "Guaranteed Minimum Rates," Bureau of the Public Debt, U.S. Savings Bond Marketing Office. To order table for present month see Chapter 17.

Table 6.4

Semi-Annual Interest Rate Bulletin

4.25% Market-Based Rate
Effective November 1993
through April 1994

Department of the Treasury
United States Savings Bonds Division
Semiannual Interest
Rate Bulletin

Cumulative Market-Based Rates

For Bonds Purchased	Bond Redeemed Nov. 1993- April 1994[4]	Bond Redeemed May- Oct. 1994[2]	Average Market- Based Rate[3]
Through April 1983[4]	7.52%	7.38%	7.38%
May - Oct. 1983	7.35%	7.21%	7.21%
Nov. 1983 - April 1984	7.50%	7.33%	7.15%
May - Oct. 1984	7.50%	7.50%	7.03%
Nov. 1984 - April 1985	7.50%	7.50%	6.88%
May - Oct. 1985	7.50%	7.50%	6.65%
Nov. 1985 - April 1986	7.50%	7.50%	6.49%
May - Oct. 1986	7.50%	7.50%	6.37%
Nov. 1986 - April 1987	6.50%	6.25%	6.33%
May - Oct. 1987	6.50%	6.25%	6.35%
Nov. 1987 - April 1988	6.50%	6.50%	6.39%
May - Oct. 1988	6.50%	6.25%	6.32%
Nov. 1988 - April 1989	6.50%	6.25%	6.27%
May - Oct. 1989		6.16%	6.16%
Nov. 1989 - April 1990	Series EE Bonds redeemed		5.97%
May - Oct. 1990	less than five years from		5.85%
Nov. 1990 - April 1991	issue earn interest at a fixed		5.68%
May - Oct. 1991	rate of 4%, compounded		5.43%
Nov. 1991 - April 1992	semiannually, if issued		5.20%
May - Oct. 1992	March 1, 1993, or later, and		4.91%
Nov. 1992 - April 1993	on a fixed, graduated scale		4.69%
May - Oct. 1993	rising from 4% six months		4.51%
Nov. 1993 - April 1994	from issue to 5.76% 4½		4.25%
	years from issue if issued		
	before March 1, 1993.		

The semiannual market-based interest rate for Series EE Bonds issued between November 1, 1993, and April 30, 1994, is 4.25% for their initial semiannual interest period. The current minimum rate is 4% for Bonds purchased on or after March 1, 1993, regardless of how long they are held, up to original maturity, a term of 18 years.

The semiannual rate changes each May and November, based on market averages during the preceding six months.

The cumulative rates in the accompanying table reflect the average of semiannual market-based interest rates applying to Bonds issued during the periods shown. The last two columns, for Bonds held through the end of semiannual periods that begin on or after November 1, 1993, include the current semiannual rate. When ten or more semiannual interest rates make up the cumulative rate, the average is applied retroactively and compounded semiannually to determine the interest rate and investment yield since the Bond's issue date (or November 1982, if later).

Series EE Bonds issued before November 1982, and all Series E Bonds and Savings Notes still earning interest, are now receiving market-based rates, or their current guaranteed rate, whichever is higher. These rates are used to calculate the redemption values of eligible Bonds for the interest accrual dates shown in the table. Future rates at redemption will reflect changes in the cumulative rate.

Series EE Savings Bonds purchased since November 1, 1982, and held five years or longer, earn the average of semiannual market-based rates during the holding period (rounded to the nearest quarter percent for those issued through April 1989) or the minimum rate in effect at the time of purchase, whichever is higher. Bonds issued prior to March 1, 1993, retain their guaranteed minimum rate through original maturity or next extended maturity.

[1] Rate used to calculate value of Bonds at interest accruals between November 1993 and April 1994. Applies from first interest date on or after November 1, 1982. Based on the average rate excluding new period, if higher than minimum.

[2] Equals last column (rounded to nearest 1/4% for maturity periods that began before May 1, 1989), or guaranteed minimum rate if higher. These rates apply to Bonds held through the end of semiannual interest periods that begin November 1, 1993, or later, and are used to calculate value of Bonds at interest accruals between May and October 1994.

[3] See other side for derivation of average rates. These averages help determine the value of Bonds at interest accruals between May and October 1994.

[4] Certain Bonds in this group yield a rate of interest other than that indicated. For details, write to address below.

U.S. Savings Bonds Division
Washington, D.C. 20226
Recorded information: 1-800-4US-BOND

Table 6.5

Interest Accrual Dates for Series E Bonds

Month of Issue May 1952 to January 1957	Interest Accrual Dates	Month of Issue June 1959 to November 1965	Interest Accrual Dates	Month of Issue June 1969 to November 1973	Interest Accrual Dates
January	March & September	January	April & October	January	May & November
February	April & October	February	May & November	February	June & December
March	May & November	March	June & December	March	July & January
April	June & December	April	July & January	April	August & February
May	July & January	May	August & February	May	September & March
June	August & February	June	September & March	June	October & April
July	September & March	July	October & April	July	November & May
August	October & April	August	November & May	August	December & June
September	November & May	September	December & June	September	January & July
October	December & June	October	January & July	October	February & August
November	January & July	November	February & August	November	March & September
December	February & August	December	March & September	December	April & October

Month of Issue February 1957 to May 1969	Interest Accrual Dates	Month of Issue December 1965 to May 1969	Interest Accrual Dates	Month of Issue December 1973 to June 1980	Interest Accrual Dates
January	June & December	January	January & July	January	January & July
February	July & January	February	February & August	February	February & August
March	August & February	March	March & September	March	March & September
April	September & March	April	April & October	April	April & October
May	October & April	May	May & November	May	May & November
June	November & May	June	June & December	June	June & December
July	December & June	July	July & January	July	July & January
August	January & July	August	August & February	August	August & February
September	February & August	September	September & March	September	September & March
October	March & September	October	October & April	October	October & April
November	April & October	November	November & May	November	November & May
December	May & November	December	December & June	December	December & June

Adapted from "Interest Accrual Dates," SBD 2082, U.S. Government Printing Office, 1993.

Table 6.6

Interest Accrual Dates for Series EE Bonds and Savings Notes

SERIES EE		SAVINGS NOTES	
Month of Issue January 1980 to February 1993. May 1995 and after.*	Interest Accrual Dates	Month of Issue May 1967 to October 1970	Interest Accrual Dates
January	January & July	January	January & July
February	February & August	February	February & August
March	March & September	March	March & September
April	April & October	April	April & October
May	May & November	May	May & November
June	June & December	June	June & December
July	July & January	July	July & January
August	August & February	August	August & February
September	September & March	September	September & March
October	October & April	October	October & April
November	November & May	November	November & May
December	December & June	December	December & June

* Series EE Bonds purchased from March 1993 to April 1995, will increase in value monthly for the first five years.
Adapted from "Interest Accrual Dates," SBD 2082, U.S. Government Printing Office, 1993.

70

Table 6.7

Tables of Redemption Values (EE)

ISSUE YEARS	MAY 1994		JUNE 1994		JULY 1994		AUGUST 1994		SEPTEMBER 1994		OCTOBER 1994		ISSUE YEARS
	ISSUE MONTHS	$50	ISSUE MONTHS	$50	ISSUE MONTHS	$50	ISSUE MONTHS	$50	ISSUE MONTHS	$50	ISSUE MONTHS	$50	
1986	Dec.	39.14	Nov.-Dec.	39.68	Nov.-Dec.	39.68	Nov.-Dec.	39.68	Nov.-Dec.	39.68	Nov.-Dec.	39.68	**1986**
	Nov.	39.68	July-Oct.	43.44	Aug.-Oct.	43.44	Sep.-Oct.	43.44	Oct.	43.44	May -Oct.	45.06	
	June-Oct.	43.44	Jan.-June	45.06	Feb.-July	45.06	Mar.-Aug.	45.06	Apr.-Sep.	45.06	Jan.-Apr.	46.76	
	Jan.-May	45.06			Jan.	46.76	Jan.-Feb.	46.76	Jan.-Mar.	46.76			
1985	Dec.	45.06	July-Dec.	46.76	Aug.-Dec.	46.76	Sep.-Dec.	46.76	Oct.-Dec.	46.76	Nov.-Dec.	46.76	**1985**
	June-Nov.	46.76	Jan.-June	48.50	Feb.-July	48.50	Mar.-Aug.	48.50	Apr.-Sep.	48.50	May -Oct.	48.50	
	Jan.-May	48.50			Jan.	50.32	Jan.-Feb.	50.32	Jan.-Mar.	50.32	Jan.-Apr.	50.32	
1984	Dec.	48.50	July-Dec.	50.32	Aug.-Dec.	50.32	Sep.-Dec.	50.32	Oct.-Dec.	50.32	Nov.-Dec.	50.32	**1984**
	June-Nov.	50.32	Jan.-June	52.22	Feb.-July	52.22	Mar.-Aug.	52.22	Apr.-Sep.	52.22	May -Oct.	52.22	
	Jan.-May	52.22			Jan.	53.28	Jan.-Feb.	53.28	Jan.-Mar.	53.28	Jan.-Apr.	53.28	
1983	Dec.	52.22	Nov.-Dec.	53.28	Nov.-Dec.	53.28	Nov.-Dec.	53.28	Nov.-Dec.	53.28	Nov.-Dec.	53.28	**1983**
	Nov.	53.28	July-Oct.	53.36	Aug.-Oct.	53.36	Sep.-Oct.	53.36	Oct.	53.36	May -Oct.	54.50	
	June-Oct.	53.36	May -June	54.50	May -July	54.50	May -Aug.	54.50	May -Sep.	54.50	Jan.-Apr.	57.54	
	May	54.50	Jan.-Apr.	56.32	Feb.-Apr.	56.32	Mar.-Apr.	56.32	Apr.	56.32			
	Jan.-Apr.	56.32			Jan.	57.54	Jan.-Feb.	57.54	Jan.-Mar.	57.54			
1982	Dec.	56.32	Nov.-Dec.	57.54	Nov.-Dec.	57.54	Nov.-Dec.	57.54	Nov.-Dec.	57.54	Nov.-Dec.	57.54	**1982**
	Nov.	57.54	July-Oct.	62.20	Aug.-Oct.	62.20	Sep.-Oct.	62.20	Oct.	62.20	May -Oct.	64.06	
	June-Oct.	62.20	Jan.-June	64.06	Feb.-July	64.06	Mar.-Aug.	64.06	Apr.-Sep.	64.06	Jan.-Apr.	65.98	
	Jan.-May	64.06			Jan.	65.98	Jan.-Feb.	65.98	Jan.-Mar.	65.98			
1981	Dec.	64.06	July-Dec.	65.98	Aug.-Dec.	65.98	Sep.-Dec.	65.98	Oct.-Dec.	65.98	Nov.-Dec.	65.98	**1981**
	June-Nov.	65.98	May -June	67.96	May -July	67.96	May -Aug.	67.96	May -Sep.	67.96	May -Oct.	67.96	
	May	67.96	Jan.-Apr.	69.60	Feb.-Apr.	69.60	Mar.-Apr.	69.60	Apr.	69.60	Jan.-Apr.	71.70	
	Jan.-Apr.	69.60			Jan.	71.70	Jan.-Feb.	71.70	Jan.-Mar.	71.70			
1980	Dec.	69.60	Nov.-Dec.	71.70	Nov.-Dec.	71.70	Nov.-Dec.	71.70	Nov.-Dec.	71.70	Nov.-Dec.	71.70	**1980**
	Nov.	71.70	July-Oct.	75.22	Aug.-Oct.	75.22	Sep.-Oct.	75.22	Oct.	75.22	May -Oct.	77.48	
	June-Oct.	75.22	May -June	77.48	May -July	77.48	May -Aug.	77.48	May -Sep.	77.48	Jan.-Apr.	79.02	
	May	77.48	Jan.-Apr.	76.72	Feb.-Apr.	76.72	Mar.-Apr.	76.72	Apr.	76.72			
	Jan.-Apr.	76.72			Jan.	79.02	Jan.-Feb.	79.02	Jan.-Mar.	79.02			

TABLES OF REDEMPTION VALUES FOR $25 SAVINGS NOTES

ISSUE YEARS	MAY 1994		JUNE 1994		JULY 1994		AUGUST 1994		SEPTEMBER 1994		OCTOBER 1994		ISSUE YEARS
	ISSUE MONTHS	$25	ISSUE MONTHS	$25	ISSUE MONTHS	$25	ISSUE MONTHS	$25	ISSUE MONTHS	$25	ISSUE MONTHS	$25	
1970	June-Oct.	103.63	July-Oct.	103.63	Aug.-Oct.	103.63	Sep.-Oct.	103.63	Oct.	103.63	July-Oct.	107.51	**1970**
	May	107.01	June	107.52	July	107.51	July-Aug.	107.51	July-Sep.	107.51	June	107.52	
	Jan.-Apr.	105.97	May	107.01	June	107.52	June	107.52	June	107.52	May	107.01	
			Jan.-Apr.	105.97	May	107.01	May	107.01	May	107.01	Jan.-Apr.	109.95	
					Feb.-Apr.	105.97	Mar.-Apr.	105.97	Apr.	105.97			
					Jan.	109.95	Jan.-Feb.	109.95	Jan.-Mar.	109.95			
1969	Dec.	105.97	Dec.	109.94	Dec.	109.94	Dec.	109.94	Dec.	109.94	Dec.	109.94	**1969**
	Nov.	109.44	Nov.	109.44	Nov.	109.44	Nov.	109.44	Nov.	109.44	Nov.	109.44	
	June-Oct.	108.39	July-Oct.	108.39	Aug.-Oct.	108.39	Sep.-Oct.	108.39	Oct.	108.39	June-Oct.	110.56	
	May	110.01	June	110.56	June-July	110.56	June-Aug.	110.56	June-Sep.	110.56	May	110.01	
	Jan.-Apr.	108.96	May	110.01	May	110.01	May	110.01	May	110.01	Jan.-Apr.	111.14	
			Jan.-Apr.	108.96	Feb.-Apr.	108.96	Mar.-Apr.	108.96	Apr.	108.96			
					Jan.	111.14	Jan.-Feb.	111.14	Jan.-Mar.	111.14			

Adapted from Tables of Redemption Values, Department of the Treasury, Bureau of the Public Debt.

Chapter 7

RECOVERING LOST BONDS

- ▸ *Replacement Is Possible*
- ▸ *Filing a Lost Bond Claim Form*
- ▸ *Bonds Found after a Replacement Has Been Issued*
- ▸ *Whether or Not to File a Form*
- ▸ *Nonreceipt Claims*

Throughout a series of seminars that the author has conducted for several chapters of American Association of Retired Persons (AARP), a common concern was encountered: "When I was in the service I remember getting those Bonds, but I don't know whatever happened to them. I assume they are gone forever and I'm out of luck." If you or a family member have Bonds that have disappeared or been destroyed, this section may help you more than any lottery.

Replacement is Possible

Any validly issued Bond that is lost, stolen, destroyed, mutilated, or not received will be replaced either by a substitute Bond bearing the same issue date or by a check

for the current redemption value, provided sufficient information and evidence in support of a claim is supplied.
—"The Book on U.S. Savings Bonds"

U.S. Savings Bonds are not like cash. If you lose money, you stand very little chance of regaining it. Savings Bonds are, however, a registered security. The government maintains records on all Bonds that have been issued and will research those records for legitimate requests *free of charge*.

There are two ways that the government classifies missing Bonds:

1. *Bonds received and subsequently lost*: The Bond owner received the Bond, but at some point in time the Bond was lost, stolen, or destroyed.

2. *Bonds purchased but never received*: A Bond was purchased, but the purchaser never received it.

Filing a Lost Bond Claim Form

If there are Bonds that you wish to locate, the first step is to get a copy of PD F 1048 ("Application for Relief on Account of Loss, Theft or Destruction of United States Savings and Retirement Securities"; Figure 7.1). This form is available from three sources: commercial banks; the Federal Reserve Bank (FRB) that services your area; and, the Bureau of the Public Debt (BPD) whose phone number is (304) 480-6112. If you attempt to obtain the form from your bank, call first to make sure they have it in stock.

It is important to note that only requests from persons who are entitled to research the Bonds will be honored. You cannot research a friend's or relative's Bonds unless you are in some way entitled and can document that entitlement.

The cover page of PD F 1048 has specific instructions for its completion and return to the BPD.

On the PD F 1048, you should give as much information as you possibly can. Here is another reason why record keeping is so important. If you have the serial numbers of the Bonds and the social security numbers of the people named on the Bonds, this will reduce search time.

If a robbery, burglary, or theft is involved, a copy of the police report should be furnished if the Bonds total $1000 (face amount) or more. Furnishing serial numbers will help speed replacement of the Bonds.

—"The Book on U.S. Savings Bonds"

A Nice Surprise for Those Who Have Lost Bonds

If you lose Bonds and replace them, there is a nice surprise in store for you. The replacement Bonds will carry the same issue date as the lost Bonds. This means that if the Bonds have not yet reached final maturity, they were earning interest the entire time they were lost. Not bad!

Bonds Found after a Replacement Has Been Issued

If a lost Bond is found after a substitute or a check has been issued, the owner must return the original Bond immediately to the Savings Bond Operations Office, with a full explanation.   *—"The Book on U.S. Savings Bonds"*

Important note: When you replace Bonds, the original Bonds become the property of the United States. If the originals are recovered, they must be surrendered for cancellation. Sometimes heirs get excited when they discover Bonds hidden in a relative's house, only to learn that the Bonds had been replaced years ago and the replacements subsequently cashed.

Whether or Not to File a Form

When in doubt, fill out the forms and have the research done. The worst-case scenario is that the Bonds to which you thought you were entitled are not found. The best-case scenario: "You're in the money!"

Allow up to a month or more for a response from the Bureau of the Public Debt. It takes a while, but they will respond to your claim eventually.

Time Limitations on Claims

> If the records show that the Bonds have been redeemed, the claim usually will be denied unless someone other than the owner or co-owner has cashed the Bonds. In such cases, an investigation of the payment may be appropriate. However, **a Bond for which no claim has been filed within ten years of the recorded date of redemption is presumed to have been properly paid.** Film records of paid Bonds are maintained for ten years following the recorded redemption date. In addition, **no claim filed six years or more after the final maturity of a Bond will be considered unless the claimant can supply its serial number.**
>
> —"The Book on U.S. Savings Bonds"

This last line is critical. Series E Bonds of the 1940s and 1950s reach final maturity forty years from the date of purchase. If you want to file a claim on a Series E Bond that is over forty-six years old, you must have the serial number.

Nonreceipt Claims

> If a Bond is not received by its purchaser or a person designated by the purchaser to receive it, the buyer should contact the organization or institution which accepted the purchase application.... —"The Book on U.S. Savings Bonds"

Now that the majority of Bonds are being issued by Federal Reserve Bank Regional Processing Sites, researching Bonds that were purchased but never received has been streamlined.

> In a case where the Bond was acquired through a Payroll Savings Plan and issued by a Federal Reserve Bank, the purchaser's employer should be informed. The Federal Reserve Bank should be notified immediately by the organization or institution through which the Bond was purchased. The Federal Reserve Bank will complete all of Part I of the claim form PD F 3062 ("Claims for Relief on Account of Loss, Theft, or Destruction of United States Savings Bonds After Valid Issue But Prior to Receipt by Owner, Co-owner or Beneficiary"). Federal Reserve Banks are expected to keep issue information for six months after Bonds are issued and provide it on a

claim form for the purchaser. The remainder of the form should then be completed and signed by all persons named on the missing Bond. Both parents should sign on behalf of a minor registrant who is too young to sign, and a court-appointed representative should sign on behalf of the estate of a deceased or incapacitated person named on the missing Bond.

If one or both parents cannot sign on behalf of a minor, or if there is no representative appointed for an estate, contact your Federal Reserve Bank. Once completed and signed, the claim form should be sent to the servicing Federal Reserve Office which issued the Bond. If a Bond was not received and more than six months have passed since that Bond was issued, the servicing Federal Reserve Bank should be contacted for instructions.

—Adapted from "The Book on U.S. Savings Bonds"

Any missing U.S. Savings Bond should be researched. If you choose not to research your Bond, and you really are entitled to it, you will never enjoy the benefits that the Bond may have provided to you. It takes a little time to file a claim, but the price is right.

Figure 7.1   **Lost Bond Claim Form (PD F 1048)**

PD F 1048
Department of the Treasury
Bureau of the Public Debt
(Revised May 1991)

APPLICATION FOR RELIEF ON ACCOUNT OF LOSS, THEFT OR DESTRUCTION OF UNITED STATES SAVINGS AND RETIREMENT SECURITIES

OMB No. 1535-0013

IMPORTANT: Follow instructions in filling out this form. You should be aware that the making of any false, fictitious or fraudulent claim to the United States is a crime punishable by imprisonment of not more than five years or a fine up to $250,000, or both, under 18 U.S.C. 287 and 18 U.S.C. 3571. Additionally, 31 U.S.C. 3729 provides for civil penalties for the maker of a false or fraudulent claim to the United States of an amount not less than $5,000 and not more than $10,000, plus treble the amount of the Government's damages as an additional sanction.
PRINT IN INK OR TYPE ALL INFORMATION

INSTRUCTIONS

("Bonds" in these instructions refers to savings bonds, savings notes, retirement plan bonds and individual retirement bonds.)

1. This form should be filled out and signed in ink.

2. (a) If the bonds are registered in the name of only one person as owner, whether or not another person has been named as beneficiary, the owner should execute Part I. If the bonds are registered in the names of two persons as coowners, Part I must be signed by both coowners and sworn to or affirmed by the one having knowledge of the facts concerning the loss, theft or destruction, except as indicated in (b). If it is not convenient for both coowners to join in one application, each should submit a separate application. If the bonds are registered in beneficiary form, the beneficiary will be required to execute PD F 1048-1, unless the beneficiary signs Part II of this application. (If any person named on the bonds is deceased, a certified copy of the death certificate must be submitted.) If the registered owner is deceased, the beneficiary should complete and sign Part I.

    (b) MINOR OWNERS, COOWNERS, OR BENEFICIARY NOT UNDER LEGAL GUARDIANSHIP. A minor owner, coowner, or beneficiary not under legal guardianship should execute this application if, in the opinion of the officer before whom the minor appears for that purpose, the minor is of sufficient competency and understanding to comprehend the nature of the transaction. Otherwise it should be executed on the minor's behalf by both parents if living, *and*, in the event the minor does not reside with either parent, also by the person who furnishes the minor's chief support. The minor's social security account number should be furnished. If any parent is unable to sign on behalf of any such minor for any reason, a statement should be provided explaining the reason why this parent is unable to sign, whether or not this parent would have had access to the bonds and whether it is believed that this parent may now have possession of the bonds.

    (c) OWNER DECEASED OR UNDER LEGAL DISABILITY. If there is a legal representative in the case of (1) a deceased owner not survived by a coowner or beneficiary, (2) a minor owner or coowner, or (3) an incapacitated owner or coowner, Part I should be executed by the representative. The representative should submit a court certificate or certified copy of letters, under seal of the court, showing that the appointment is still in force, unless his/her name and official capacity appear on the bonds, in which case no evidence of the appointment will ordinarily be required. If there is no legal representative in the case of a deceased owner or incompetent owner, the Department of the Treasury should be fully informed as to the facts so that further instructions may be given.

3. *If any person other than the applicant had custody or possession of the bonds at the time of loss, theft or destruction or has firsthand knowledge of the circumstances under which the bonds were lost, stolen or destroyed, the applicant should have such person furnish a statement on Part II of this form or a separate supporting affidavit. If the space provided in Part II is not sufficient in any particular case, the statement should be continued on a separate sheet which should be attached hereto.*

4. Part I (and Part II when required by Instruction 3.) must be signed before an authorized certifying officer or before a notary public or other officer authorized by law to administer oaths for general purposes. Authorized certifying officers are available at banking institutions, including credit unions, in the United States, and as further provided in the current revisions of Department of the Treasury Circular No. 530 and Public Debt Series, Nos. 1-63, 1-75 and 3-80. A certifying officer must impress or imprint the seal or stamp which he/she is required to use in certifying requests for payment. A notary public or similar officer must impress his/her official seal and show the expiration date of his/her commission.

5. If any investigation of the loss or theft was made by the police or other local law enforcement agency or by any insurance, transportation or similar business organization, please attach to this form a copy of the report of such agency.

6. Ordinarily a substitute bond or check will be issued as soon as practicable after the Bureau of the Public Debt receives a report of the loss, theft or destruction. However, if its records disclose that the bonds have been cashed and it becomes necessary to refer the case to the United States Secret Service for investigation, substitute bonds or a check will not be issued until the investigation is completed.

7. The application and correspondence relating thereto should be sent to the Bureau of the Public Debt, Parkersburg, West Virginia 26106-1328.

8. The applicant should make and retain a copy of this form, or some other statement, with other important papers. This record should serve as a reminder to the applicant and to others who may have occasion to take care of the applicant's affairs that when relief is granted on account of lost, stolen or destroyed bonds, the original bonds become the property of the United States and must be surrendered to the Department for cancellation if they are recovered.

Figure 7.1 Lost Bond Claim Form (PD F 1048) continued

PART I

The undersigned hereby severally affirm and say that the following-described bonds have been lost, stolen or destroyed and that the information given herein is true to the best of their knowledge and belief: (If application is made on account of destroyed bonds, any charred, scorched or undestroyed pieces should be submitted herewith.)

ISSUE DATE	DENOMINATION (FACE AMOUNT)	SERIAL NUMBER	INSCRIPTION (Please type or print names, including middle names or initials, social security account number, if any, and addresses as inscribed on the bonds.)

(If space is insufficient, use a continuation sheet, sign it, and refer to it above. PD F 3500 may be used for this purpose.)

1. Are you the registered owner of the bonds? _____ If so, go to number 6., unless a minor is named on the bond with you. If a minor is named on the bond, go to number 5.

2. If you are not the registered owner, in what capacity are you acting? _____ (See Instruction 2.)

3. If you are acting as guardian or legal representative, have you been court appointed? _____ [See Instruction 2. (c)]

4. What is your relationship to the registered owner? _____

5. If you are acting on behalf of a minor for whose estate there is no court-appointed guardian or other representative and the minor is not of sufficient competency and understanding to complete the questions in this application, answer the following questions: [See Instruction 2. (b)]

   (a) What is the minor's age _____ , Social Security Number _____ and your relationship to the minor? _____

   (b) Does the minor live with you? _____ If not, give the name and address of the person with whom he/she lives _____ .

   (c) If you are not the father or mother of the minor, who furnishes his/her chief support? _____
   _____

6. (a) Were the bonds (1) lost? _____ (2) stolen? _____ (date of theft) _____ or (3) destroyed? _____ (See Instruction 5.)

   (b) On what date was this discovered? _____

   (c) Who had them last, and for what purpose? (See Instruction 3.) _____

   _____

   _____

79

Figure 7.1 **Lost Bond Claim Form (PD F 1048)** continued

(d) Give the result of inquiry made of other persons as to their knowledge of the loss, theft or destruction of the bonds. (E.g., who, besides you, had access to the bonds, where were they last placed, and on what date were they last seen?) _____

_____

_____

(e) List any identification documents (i.e., driver's license) lost or stolen with the bonds. _____

_____

7. (a) Has the owner, or anyone on the owner's behalf, received reimbursement from any source on account of the loss, theft or destruction of the bonds? _____

(b) If any reimbursement has been received, explain fully. _____

_____

_____

8. Do you wish: (a) bonds _____ or (b) a check _____ ? If you wish a check and the bonds are in the names of living coowners, state the name of the coowner to whom the check is to be drawn. Otherwise, the check will be drawn to both coowners and the entire interest reported under the first-named coowner's social security number.

_____

_____

(Series EE and HH savings bonds are not eligible for payment until six months from their issue dates.)

9. Mail bonds or check to: Name _____

Address _____
  (Number and street or rural route)   (City or town)   (State)   (ZIP Code)

    We, the undersigned, hereby severally petition the Secretary of the Treasury for relief as authorized by law, and if such relief is granted, hereby acknowledge that the original bonds shall thereupon become the property of the United States. Upon the granting of relief, we assign all our right, title and interest in the original bonds to the United States and hereby bind ourselves, our heirs, executors, administrators, successors, and assigns, jointly and severally: (1) to surrender the original bonds to the Department of the Treasury should they be recovered; (2) to hold the United States harmless on account of any claim by any other parties having, or claiming to have, interests in these bonds; and, (3) upon demand by the Department of the Treasury, to indemnify unconditionally the United States and to repay to the Department of the Treasury all sums of money which the Department may pay on account of the redemption of these original bonds, including any interest, administrative costs and penalties and any other liability or losses incurred as a result of such redemption. The undersigned hereby consent to the release of any information contained herein, or regarding the bonds described herein, to any party having an ownership or entitlement interest in these bonds.

Signature _____   Signature _____
              (Name)   (Name)

Home
Address_____   Address _____
        (Number and street or rural route)   (Number and street or rural route)

(City or town)   (State)   (ZIP Code)   (City or town)   (State)   (ZIP Code)

☐☐☐ – ☐☐ – ☐☐☐☐   ☐☐☐ – ☐☐ – ☐☐☐☐
Social Security Account Number   Social Security Account Number

☐☐☐ – ☐☐☐☐ – ☐☐☐☐   ☐☐☐ – ☐☐☐☐ – ☐☐☐☐
Daytime Telephone Number   Daytime Telephone Number

THE CERTIFICATION AT THE TOP OF THE NEXT PAGE MUST BE COMPLETED. SEE INSTRUCTIONS 2. (a) AND 4. ON PAGE 1.

_____
_____ Chapter 8

TAXATION ISSUES FOR
U.S. SAVINGS BONDS
a.k.a. What Uncle Sam Wants

- ▸ *Common Tax Mistakes*
- ▸ *How and When to Report Interest Income*
- ▸ *Who Has to Report Interest Income*
- ▸ *Tax Concerns when Transferring Bonds*
- ▸ *Taxes upon Death*
- ▸ *Watch Out for Double Taxation*
- ▸ *Federal Estate Tax*
- ▸ *Gift and Inheritance Taxes*

Tax information.... A typical chapter on this exhilarating subject will cure even the worst case of insomnia. And quite frankly, this chapter contains quite a bit of technical information. However, you will find some things that catch your attention: tax tips; how to avoid tax traps; and information designed to help you recognize your options.

Due to the specific nature of this chapter, there is more technical language here than in other parts of this book. This change in style is necessary to thoroughly address these very important tax issues. The information presented in this chapter relies in large part upon the

Internal Revenue Service Publications 17 and 550 and the Department of Treasury, Bureau of the Public Debt, "Legal Aspects of U.S. Savings Bonds" and "The Book on U.S. Savings Bonds."

In many cases, publications carry similar information. Throughout this chapter, whenever possible, a reader-friendly explanation accompanies the technical explanation.

Since March 1, 1941, the interest on U.S. Savings Bonds has been subject to federal income tax, but exempt from state, municipal, or local income taxes.

Common Tax Mistakes

When evaluating the status of your Savings Bond holdings, taxation issues should be taken into careful consideration. This will ensure that you receive the maximum total return on your Bond investment. Here are four of the most common tax mistakes Bond owners make:

Mistake #1: Cashing Savings Bonds without first considering how much interest income will be reported and how much tax liability must be paid.

Mistake #2: Gifting or transferring Bonds without knowing the tax consequences.

Mistake #3: Paying double tax: Unknowingly paying tax again on Bond interest that had already been reported.

Mistake #4: Lower-income retired persons cashing a large number of Bonds in one year, causing a large portion of their Social Security benefits to be taxable.

How and When to Report Interest Income

In order to determine how interest on Savings Bonds is taxed, two questions must be answered:

1. Is the taxpayer using the cash basis or accrual basis of accounting for income tax purposes?

2. What type of Savings Bond is being analyzed (E, EE, SN, H, HH)?

Cash Basis-Accounting vs. Accrual Basis

The cash basis of accounting is used by the majority of individuals owning U.S. Savings Bonds. If you don't know whether you are on the cash or accrual method, most likely you are on the cash method. You must expend effort to elect the accrual method; if you have never specifically elected accrual, the cash method is the automatic *default*.

The difference between the purchase price of an E or EE Bond and its redemption value is considered interest income under IRS Code. At some point in time, this income will have to be reported. When to include (or report) this interest income in taxable income (on a tax return) becomes an important issue. Interest on Series E and EE Bonds and SN is not paid on an annual or semi-annual basis to the Bond holder. Instead, the interest is added to the value of the Bond and is paid when the Bond is cashed. This is called interest accrual: The Bond value is growing as a result of the interest being added to the value of the Bond. The taxpayer on the cash basis must choose between two methods of reporting interest income.

1. **Deferral**. Defer the reporting of the interest income until the year in which the E or EE Bonds or SN are cashed, disposed of, or reach final maturity, whichever comes first. If you do nothing, this is the option you have chosen. All the interest accrued will be reported in the year the Bonds are cashed or reach final maturity.

2. **Annual Reporting**. Report the interest earned each year as it accrues on the Bond.

Deferral

When you buy a Bond and do nothing about the interest, you have automatically chosen the deferral method. The interest the Bond is earning causes the Bond to increase in value, but you choose not to be taxed annually on the interest because none of this income has been received in the form of cash. It should be emphasized that when the Bonds are cashed under this method, all the interest earned on the Bond will be taxable in one year.

For older Bonds, this could result in a significant amount of taxable income in one year. There have been many instances when a taxpayer cashed Bonds without taking into account the *timing* of the transaction for income tax purposes, looking only at the interest rates and liquidity issues. With proper tax planning, cashing Bonds can be timed to minimize tax liability. This is especially important if the taxpayer has had an unusually high- or low-income year.

TAX TRAP: When a Bond reaches final maturity, it not only stops accruing interest but any interest accrued is taxable that year. This is an easy item to overlook since Bond owners receive no statement telling them that a particular Bond has stopped earning interest. Thus many Bond owners unknowingly hold Bonds after they reach final maturity. If you hold Bonds that are over three years past final maturity, consult a professional tax advisor for your options.

If you discover this situation after your tax returns for that year have been filed, amended returns should be filed to properly report the Bond interest income. It is extremely important to know when your Bonds are scheduled to reach final maturity so you can plan for the tax impact on the interest that has accrued on each Bond.

Series E Bonds issued before December 1965 reach final maturity forty years after their issue date. Series E Bonds issued after November 1965 and all Series EE Bonds and Savings Notes reach final maturity thirty years after their issue date. **Note**: A special rule permits further deferral if an E Bond or Savings Note is exchanged for Series HH Bonds no later than one calendar year after the Bond reaches final maturity.

> A $1,000 Series E Bond purchased in 1954 for $750 has a current value of about $7,000. If the owner has not already reported any of the interest on this Bond, the entire difference of $6,250 is potentially taxable as interest income in 1994. The only way to avoid the liability in 1994 is to exchange for HH Bonds.

TAX TIP: Taxpayers holding Series E Bonds that are reaching final maturity should consider whether they want all the interest income taxed in the year of final maturity. If they do not, they should consider exchanging their Series E for HH Bonds. The interest on the HH Bonds is paid every six months and is taxable in the year of receipt. However, the accrued interest on the Series E Bonds that have been surrendered will continue to be deferred until the Series HH Bonds are either cashed or mature (see Chapter 10 for details on exchanging).

Annual Reporting

Under the "cash basis" method, the holder of the Bond may choose to report the annual increase in the value of the Bond (the interest income) in each year's tax return rather than waiting until the Bond is cashed or reaches final maturity.

If a taxpayer wants to report the interest as it accrues, *all* interest accrued and not previously reported on all Series E and EE Bonds and SN must be included as income for the tax year in which this election is made (that is, the year you start to report interest annually). In other words, if a taxpayer chooses this method, it will apply to all the Bonds he or she owns. You cannot pick and choose the Bonds you want to report annual interest on and leave the rest alone. It should be kept in mind that once you choose to report the interest each year, you must continue to do so for all Series E and EE Bonds and SN you own and for any you obtain later, unless you request permission from the IRS to change back to the deferral method. (See IRS Publication 17 for rules on changing methods.)

If the taxpayer is in a low tax bracket, it may make sense to be taxed on the interest income each year as it accrues. In some situations, little or no tax is paid if the income is reported each year. If all the income is taxed in the year the Bonds are cashed or in the year of final maturity, this "bunching" of the interest income may create a significantly higher total tax than if the tax had been paid each year. This would be especially true for a low-income taxpayer who held a large number of Bonds which would come due in one tax year.

For example, a seventy-year old single taxpayer has Bonds that are increasing in value at $3,000 per year. The taxpayer also has $5,000 of additional taxable interest income and receives $10,000 in Social Security benefits each year. She plans to cash the Bonds in ten years.

> *Option 1*: She decides to report as interest income the $3,000 per year as the Bonds increase in value. The total federal income tax due each year using 1994 rates and exemptions would total $120 per year, for a total federal income tax of $1,200 for the ten years.

> *Option 2*: She chooses to defer the interest income on these Bonds and pick up the whole $30,000 ($3,000 times 10 years) in year ten. The total federal income tax due would then be approximately $7,200, assuming that the tax rates are similar to 1994 rates.

In this simple situation, the difference in total federal income tax between options 1 and 2 is *$6,000*. This is a considerable amount of money that the taxpayer could enjoy. *The time value of money must be taken into account when making this calculation* since the taxes in option 1 are being paid earlier than in option 2. In this case, however, the difference is so great that it is still much better to prepay the smaller amount each year than to defer it until year ten.

TAX TRAP: In the situation above, part of the increase in tax occurs in year ten when all the Bond interest income is taxable. A portion of her Social Security benefits would become taxable, too, because she has a higher total income. This tax bite surprises many a taxpayer who is receiving Social Security and cashes in a large amount of Bonds without considering this factor. In the example above, $2,380 of the $6,000 additional taxes was due to the fact that $8,500 of the $10,000 Social Security benefits received that year were taxed because of the influx of all that Bond interest.

When you choose the annual reporting methods for a minor, the first year's tax return should report all the interest income accrued through that tax year. In successive years the minor need only file if his or her total income exceeds the IRS level. In 1993, a minor who made less than $600 did not need to file. If you choose this method, please pay special attention to the double taxation discussion later in this chapter to ensure that you avoid reporting the interest twice.

Accrual Basis: E and EE Bonds

If the taxpayer has specifically elected the accrual basis for income tax purposes, the interest on E and EE Bonds *must be reported as income each year* as the interest accrues.

H and HH Bonds

Interest on Series H and HH Bonds is paid semi-annually by check or by direct deposit and must be reported annually for federal income tax purposes.

Who Has to Report
Interest Income

Co-owners

When Bonds are held by co-owners, there is often a great deal of confusion as to who is liable for the tax on the interest when the Bond is redeemed. The following chart adopted from the "Legal Aspects On U.S. Savings Bonds" states the government's position. As discussed in Chapter 13, the actual reporting method used by the banks, Federal Reserve Banks (FRB), and IRS when documenting Social Security numbers and names to generate a 1099-INT *does not* match the rules outlined:

Bond Purchaser	**Tax Liability**
"Dad" buys Bond in the names of "Dad" and "Son" as co-owners.	Interest is income to "Dad," the person who contributed the purchase price.
"Dad" and "Son" buy Bonds in co-ownership, with each contributing part of the purchase price.	Interest is income to both "Dad" and "Son," in proportion to their contributions to the purchase price.
"Son" and "Daughter" receive Bonds in co-ownership as gift from "Dad."	Interest is income to both "Son" and "Daughter": 50% to each co-owner.
"Mom" buys a Bond in the name of "Son," who is the sole owner of the Bond.	Interest is income to "Son."

If you buy a U.S. Savings Bond and add a co-owner, the person whose funds were used to purchase the Bond is the person who must pay the tax on the interest. This is true even if the purchaser lets the other co-owner redeem the Bond and keep the proceeds.

The problem with this situation is that the organization that redeems the Bonds will issue a 1099-INT to the person who redeems the Bond despite the fact that, according to IRS rules, the interest is taxable to the co-owner who purchased the Bond. Since the redeeming co-owner will receive a 1099-INT at the time of redemption, he or she is supposed to provide the purchaser/co-owner (who is to be taxed) with another 1099-INT, showing the amount of interest that is taxable.

The co-owner who redeemed the Bond is called a "nominee." If a taxpayer receives a 1099-INT for interest received as a "nominee," he or she should list that amount separately below the subtotal of all interest income listed on Schedule B. That amount should be labeled "Nominee Distribution" and subtracted from the interest income subtotal. This procedure ensures that the Bond interest will not be added into the "nominee's" taxable income on his or her tax return.

Author's note: If the previous section seems confusing, don't be alarmed: It is absolutely confusing. The purpose of this chapter is to inform you of the rules—whether they make sense, are being enforced, or even have the capacity to be enforced. The author is not aware of a single case in which the redeeming, nonpurchaser co-owner actually issued a 1099-INT to the first-named co-owner and sent a copy to IRS.

This rule leaves room for shady action, as you may realize. According to this rule, Uncle John buys Bonds with his nephew as a co-owner. His nephew cashes the Bonds and receives a 1099-INT. The young man then turns around and issues a 1099-INT to Uncle John and reports that same 1099-INT to IRS. Nephew is now "in the money" tax-free. The only drawback may be meeting up with his uncle in the near future.

Tax Concerns when Transferring Bonds

There are many situations when Bonds are reissued to a different person's name or are reissued to eliminate, or add, a co-owner's name. The question that is often overlooked by the taxpayer and the financial advisor making these changes is "Does this change cause tax consequences to any of the parties involved?" The answer could be "yes" or "no," depending on the situation. Each time a change in ownership due to the reissue of Bonds is recommended, tax consequences must be considered.

Nontaxable Event

The general rule is that *a change in the registration of a Savings Bond that does not change ownership will not result in shifting income tax liability.* Here are some examples when changes *do not* result in the shifting of income tax liability and consequently are *not* considered a disposition that requires the owner to include the accrued or previously unreported interest on the Bond in his or her gross income.

1. The original owner who furnished 100% of the funds to purchase the Bond has it reissued to name the original owner and another person as co-owner.

2. An original owner who furnished 100% of the funds for the Bond's purchase has the Bond reissued to eliminate a co-owner's name from the Bond.

3. If Bonds that two co-owners purchased jointly are reissued to each of the co-owners in the same proportion as their original contribution to the purchase price, neither of the co-owners has to report, at reissue, the interest earned before the Bonds were reissued.

4. The owner can continue to postpone reporting the interest earned if a taxpayer owns Series E or EE Bonds and
    a. transfers them to a trust,
    b. is considered the owner of the trust, and
    c. the increase in value both before and after the transfer continues to be taxable to the owner.

5. If a person who owns Series EE Bonds exchanges them for Series HH Bonds, and the Series HH Bonds are issued in the owner's name and that of another co-owner, there are two conditions that must be met in order for this to be a nontaxable event. First, the person who was the original owner must remain the owner. Second, the original owner must include in his or her income all the interest on the new Series HH Bonds in the year the payments are received.

Taxable Event

What action creates a taxable event? These following situations illustrate when a change in registration will cause the interest to become taxable at the time of the change.

1. If a person buys Series E or EE Bonds entirely with his own funds and has them reissued in a co-owner's name alone, this is considered a disposition. In the year of reissue the original Bond purchaser must report all the interest earned on these Bonds that has not been previously reported.

2. If a person buys Series E or EE Bonds entirely with his or her own funds and has them reissued in another beneficiary's name alone, this is considered a disposition. In the year of reissue, the original Bond purchaser must report all the interest earned on these Bonds that has not been previously reported.

3. When a person who owns Series E or EE Bonds gives the Bonds to another person and reissues the Bonds in the recipient's name alone, the reissuance of the Bonds causes this to be a taxable situation for the person who makes the gift. Any previously unreported interest would have to be included in the giver's income in the year of the reissue. **Note**: Any interest earned on the Bond after the reissue would be taxable to the person who received the gift.

4. If a person transfers Series E or EE Bonds to a trust and also gives up all rights of ownership, that person must report all the

interest earned through the date of transfer (that has not been previously reported). This interest would be taxable in the year of transfer.

Additional Note: Be aware that persons who inherit Bonds may create taxable events by removing their names from the Bonds. Contact your FRB or a professional tax advisor for more information before taking a course of action.

Taxes upon Death

Many financial professionals and Bond owners expect that, like other investment vehicles, a stepped-up basis should apply to all U.S. Savings Bonds. This is *not* the case. In fact, there is no automatic stepped-up basis for people who inherit or receive Bonds upon the death of another individual.

The manner of reporting interest income on Series E or EE Bonds after the death of the owner depends on the accounting and income reporting method the decedent had used. If the Bonds transferred at death were owned by a person who used the accrual method (or who used the cash method and chose to report the interest each year), the interest earned in the year of death must be reported on that person's final return. The person who acquires the Bonds includes as income only interest earned after the date of death.

If the decedent had used the cash basis method (and had not reported the interest each year) and had bought the Bonds entirely with his or her own funds, all interest earned before death must be reported in one of the following ways:

1. The surviving spouse or personal representative (executor, administrator, etc.) who files the final income tax return of the decedent can choose to include on that return all of the interest earned on the Bonds before the decedent's death. The person who acquires the Bonds then includes as income only interest earned after the date of death

2. If you do not choose option 1 the interest earned up to the date of death is *income in respect of a decedent* and it should not be included in the decedent's final return. *All of the interest earned both before and after the decedent's death is income to the person who acquires the Bonds.* If that person uses the cash method and chooses not to report the interest each year, he or she can postpone reporting any of the interest until the Bonds are redeemed or reach final maturity, whichever comes first. In the year that the interest

is reported, he or she can claim a deduction for any federal estate tax paid that was for the part of the interest that was included in the decedent's estate.

In summary, the personal representative of the estate actually has three options.

1. Elect to report unreported Savings Bond interest on the final income tax return of the decedent under Code Section 454(a) of the Internal Revenue Code.

2. Report all of the Savings Bond interest in the estate. This can be done by electing to report all previously unreported interest in the estate or by reporting the interest as the Bonds are cashed in the estate.

3. Distribute the Bonds to the residuary beneficiaries (the person or persons entitled to the estate residue, whatever is left over from the estate assets and not specifically designated to a particular entity). In this case, the beneficiaries would report the Savings Bond interest when cashed or in the year an election is made to report previously unreported interest.

It should be noted that beneficiaries who receive Bonds can choose to continue deferring interest or report interest annually on the Bonds they receive.

TAX TIP: To see which option provides the lowest amount of federal income tax liability when a large number of Bonds are involved, the tax consequences for all three options must be calculated. If the decedent was in a low income bracket, it often makes sense to include the interest in the decedent's final return.

Watch Out for Double Taxation

Can Savings Bond interest be double taxed by the Internal Revenue Service? You bet it can! While not intentional, it nonetheless happens often due to the confusing nature of the rules. As mentioned earlier, the financial institution that redeems the Bond will issue a 1099-INT to the person redeeming it. The 1099-INT shows the difference between the amount the holder receives and the purchase price. **Important note**: There are several instances when the 1099-INT may show more interest than the taxpayer is required to include as income on the tax return. This may happen if:

1.   You chose to report the increase in the redemption value of the Bond each year. The interest shown on your 1099-INT will not be reduced by the amounts previously included in income.

2.   You received a Bond from a decedent. The interest shown on your 1099-INT will not be reduced by the interest reported by the decedent before death, or on the decedent's final return, or by the estate on the estate's income tax return.

3.   The interest shown on your 1099-INT will not be reduced by the interest accrued prior to a transfer of Bond ownership.

4.   You redeemed a Bond on which you were named as a co-owner but which you did not buy; the person who had purchased the Bonds previously reported interest accrued.

TAX TIP: Any taxpayer or personal representative who chooses to include interest on U.S. Savings Bonds in a year other than the year the Bonds are redeemed should keep a detailed worksheet showing the years when the interest was taxed, as well as the amount of interest that was previously included as income. They should also keep copies of the federal tax returns (Form 1040 and Schedule B) on which this interest was reported. These records should be safely stored and available to the co-owners and to persons who may obtain the Bonds through reissue transactions.

TAX TIP: If you have received a sizable number of Bonds from a decedent and have paid tax on the interest for the entire 1099-INT issued, check prior records to see if any of this income had been previously taxed in the decedent's tax returns or in the estate returns. *If this has happened within the past three years, you may be entitled to a federal income tax refund and should file amended returns.* Better yet, now that you know what to look for, research the reported interest status of your Bonds before you cash them.

Federal Estate Tax

In this section, we will not go into a deep discussion of estate tax rules. We will only discuss issues relating to U.S. Savings Bonds. Much of the information in the next few sections is technical and is adapted from the Bureau of the Public Debt's (BPD) publication, "The Book On U.S. Savings Bonds."

To begin, one must understand that the estate is primarily liable for any estate tax that can be attributed to Bonds that were owned by the decedent, even if they pass directly to a co-owner or beneficiary. In the event the estate fails to pay the estate tax, the persons receiving the Bonds or other property could be required to pay the estate tax.

Determining Bond Values

When Savings Bonds are included for estate tax calculation purposes, it is important to include the proper value of the Bonds. The proper value is the redemption value of the Bond on the date of the owner's death. An increasing number of personal representatives and legal counsel are engaging the services of The Savings Bond Informer, Inc., rather than tracking down old redemption tables and calculating the value of each Bond themselves. (See Chapter 6, "Tracking Your Investment.")

Income Tax Deduction for Federal Estate Tax Paid

Under certain conditions, it is possible for a taxpayer to take a deduction for federal estate tax paid on Savings Bond interest that was included in a decedent's estate for tax calculation purposes. Assume, for example, that the taxpayer acquired the Bonds either as surviving co-owner, beneficiary, or distributee of an estate of a (cash basis) taxpayer who had not elected to report interest annually. At the time the accrued interest on the Bonds is reported as income, the taxpayer would be entitled to claim a deduction on his or her federal income tax return for the portion of the estate tax paid that was applicable as a result of interest accrued during the decedent's lifetime.

It should be emphasized that this is not a dollar-for-dollar offset. It is a deduction that may or may not equalize the taxes, depending on the respective tax brackets of the estate and the income distributee. The computations in this area can be very complicated: Consult a tax advisor.

Gift and Inheritance Taxes

Federal Gift Tax

Any one taxpayer who gives more than $10,000 to any other person in a calendar year must file a gift tax return (Form 709). The value of any U.S. Savings Bonds given would be included in this $10,000 computation. The value used for the gift would be the redemption value on the date of the gift. A gift of Savings Bonds can be made in several ways and is subject to the federal gift tax.

One way to give Savings Bonds is to purchase the Bonds in the name of the person who will receive them (the donee). Another way is to reissue the Bonds in the name of the donee. If the value of the Bonds given is under $10,000 per year per donee, there is no gift tax. If gifts of more than $10,000 are made in one year to one person, gift tax is due. *The tax is imposed on the person making the gift*, not the person receiving the gift.

A husband and wife may combine their gift tax-exemptions to give a third person a total of $20,000. The husband could give $20,000 in Savings Bonds to the third person without exceeding each spouse's $10,000 annual exemption. Both the husband and wife must consent to the gift-splitting by signing gift tax Form 709, which must be filed for the year the gift is given.

State Gift Tax

U.S. Savings Bonds are not subject to state gift tax.

State Inheritance Tax

When Bond ownership is transferred by the death of one owner, it is subject to state inheritance tax. For the case of co-owned Bonds, many states follow the rule applied under the federal estate tax provisions—measuring each co-owner's taxable interest by the amount each contributed to the purchase price. Other states view the Bonds as held in equal shares by each co-owner and require that one-half of their value be reported as part of the gross estate of the co-owner first to die, regardless of who purchased the Bonds. Contact the tax authorities for your state for current information.

The information in this chapter is based on current tax laws. Be aware that tax laws are constantly changing and that the information in these pages may become obsolete. It is not the intent to offer legal or tax advice. The author strongly suggests any person with a specific Savings Bond tax issue or legal issue, consult a competent and experienced tax and/or legal professional for advice.

Chapter 9

THE EDUCATIONAL FEATURE
OF SERIES EE BONDS

▸ *Common Misconceptions*
▸ *What the Advertising Did Not Cover*
▸ *Conditions for Qualifying for the Tax-Free Status*
▸ *Record Keeping for the Educational Feature*
▸ *Will the Current Interest Rates Be Enough?*
▸ *Pros and Cons of the Educational Feature*
▸ *An Alternative for Reducing the Tax Burden*

What you have heard is true: The largest single expenditure you will ever make, other than buying a home, will most likely be your child's college tuition. By the first decade of the twenty-first century, if recent inflation rates hold, four years at an in-state public institution will cost at least $86,000, and four years at a private college will total about $163,000.

> —Janet Bamford, "The Class of 2013," *Sesame Street Parents* (September 1994), pp. 52-55.

With educational costs skyrocketing, many parents are paying increased attention to investment options to pay for their children's future tuition. This is certainly true in the author's state, whose public universities announced average tuition hikes of 8 to 10% for the coming year. The educational feature of the Series EE Bond has received a lot of media attention. A closer examination will enable you to assess whether it is right for you.

Common Misconceptions

"Tax-Free for Education." In the early 1990s you probably heard the radio advertisements pitch the sale of EE Bonds for the purpose of saving for a college education. Here are the most common misunderstandings.

Misconception #1: *All Bonds are now tax-free if used for education.*

No. There is an abundance of misinformation on this point. Only Series EE Bonds purchased as of January 1, 1990, are eligible, and then only if *eight* other conditions have been met. A complete list of the conditions is presented later in this chapter.

Misconception #2: *I must buy the Bonds in my child's name so I can use them tax-free for education.*

No. Buying Bonds in your child's name is not necessarily a bad idea, as you will see in the latter part of this chapter. However, if you do buy a Bond in your child's name, you have just eliminated that Bond from being eligible for the tax-free educational feature. If you have already registered your Bonds this way because someone gave you inaccurate information, you can retitle the Bond. Call your regional Federal Reserve Bank (see Chapter 17, "U.S. Savings Bond Resources"), explain the situation, and ask for the appropriate reissue form.

Misconception #3: *I'm buying Bonds in the name of my grandchildren so they can use the tax-free educational feature.*

No. Grandparents have to purchase the Bonds in the name of the *parents* of their grandchildren if the plan is to qualify the Bonds for the tax-free educational feature. This could be risky business in some families: The parents may not honor the wishes of the grandparents concerning the intent of the Bonds. Since they are named on the Bonds, the parents may negotiate the Bonds at their own discretion. However, if properly used by all involved, this can be a way for grandparents to contribute to their grandchildren's education.

Misconception #4: *At the time of purchase, I have to declare that the Bonds will be used for education.*

No. You do not have to declare your intent with any Bond purchase. You can buy the Bonds with the intent of using them for education and then change your mind. Cashing them for another purpose means you forfeit the opportunity for the Bonds to be "tax-free for education," but there are no additional penalties or hidden fees.

What the Advertising Did Not Cover

Most of the misconceptions that Bond owners have about the educational feature of the Series EE Bond were the result of brief media announcements or advertisements. Regardless of the cause, many who bought Bonds because "they are now tax-free for education" were unhappy to learn that they did not know "the rest of the story." And they are not alone. Unfortunately, the ill-advised and unknowledgeable are perpetuating these inaccuracies.

What is the "rest of the story"? For starters you need to know the conditions that must be met to qualify for the tax-free status.

Conditions for Qualifying for the Tax-Free Status

There are eight conditions, which must be met in order to qualify for the tax-free feature of EE Bonds. The conditions, from the government publication "U.S. Savings Bonds: Now Tax-Free for Education," are:

1. Only EE Bonds purchased after December 31, 1989, qualify.

2. The Bonds must be registered in the name of either one or both of the parents. The child cannot be listed on the Bond as owner or co-owner. However, the child can be listed on the Bond as the POD (pay on death) recipient.

3. The parents must be at least twenty-four years of age when purchasing the Bonds. *Author's note: Please don't ask me why.*

4. The income of the parents *in the year the Bond is cashed* will determine whether the Bond is exempt from federal tax. (U.S. Bonds are always exempt from state and local taxes.) In 1990, this was set at $60,000 for a married couple filing jointly and $40,000 for a single parent. A partial tax break was available (up to $90,000) for a married couple filing jointly. These income limits are supposedly indexed to inflation each year, and, in fact, had been until 1993. In 1993, the annual bill to increase the income limit for the educational feature carried the wrong "base year" for calculation, thus throwing the limit back to the 1990 standard. An amendment to correct this and reestablish income limits that abide by the rules under which the Bonds were sold is under consideration for 1995. Contact the Bureau of the Public Debt for the current year income limits. Chapter 17 contains the address and phone number.

5. Bonds must be redeemed the same year that the Bond owner pays his, her, or their child's educational expenses to an eligible institution.

6. The only expenses to which Bonds can be applied are tuition and fees. Room, board, and books do not qualify.

7. Educational institutions that are eligible include colleges, universities, technical institutes, and vocational schools located in the United States.

8. The interest on Bonds that qualify for the educational feature can be excluded from federal income tax only if the redemption proceeds (interest and principal) are less than or equal to the qualifying tuition and fees paid during the year. If the value of the Bonds cashed is greater than the eligible tuition and fees, a proportional amount of the Bond interest is exempt. That is, if the tuition and fees total $5,000, yet you redeem $20,000 of eligible Bonds, only 25% of the interest income can be excluded from federal income tax.

Additional rule for married couples: Couples who wish to use the educational feature tax exclusion must file a joint return.

Record Keeping for the Educational Feature

According to the Treasury Department, Bureau of the Public Debt, Bond owners should keep specific records on EE Bonds that qualify for the educational feature. For each Bond you should have the following:

✓ Serial numbers
✓ Face value
✓ Issue date
✓ Date of redemption
✓ Total proceeds received (principal and interest)

In addition, you will need to document:

✓ The name of the educational institution that received payment
✓ The date the expenses were paid
✓ The amount of qualified expenses

Forms 8815 and 8818 are both appropriate IRS forms for recording your transaction. Figures 9.1 and 9.2 provide copies of these forms.

To avoid duplication in record keeping, please note that several of the items mentioned above are already a part of your Bond records if you followed the suggestions in Chapter 5, "Organizing Your Bonds." (Additional information is presented in Chapter 6, "Tracking Your Investment.")

Will the Current Interest Rates Be Enough?

Good question. And here is where the debate really heats up. The author is neither a financial planner nor a financial advisor, but he has heard plenty of views on whether interest rates on Bonds will "cut the mustard."

The guaranteed rate for Bonds purchased between March 1993 to April 1995 is 4%. At 4%, a Bond will take eighteen years to reach face value or double. This means if Junior was born yesterday and somehow makes it through high school by age eighteen, the Bonds purchased at his birth will be worth double the purchase price by the time Junior starts college. Um...not exactly bowled over yet?

There is an upside potential. If the average variable rate on the Bonds exceeds 4% and the Bonds are held for at least five years, then this higher rate will be realized. For example, if the average variable rate is 6% after the first twelve years of the Bond's life, then the Bond will reach face value (or double) in only twelve years. That may be better, but is it good enough?

"**New Rules**": Effective May 1, 1995, new purchases of EE Bonds will be assigned a different market-based rate for every six-month period over the life of the Bond. How quickly will your money grow?

That depends on market conditions and the individual rates that are published and assigned to your Bond. Table 9.1 shows approximately how long it will take your money to double at a given interest rate. Remember though that your rates will not be constant under the new rules. The rates will fluctuate up and down, tied to either six-month Treasury yields (if your Bond is less than five years old) or to five-year Treasury yields (if your Bond is held five years or longer). If the rates average 6%, your money will double in twelve years. If the rates average 4%, your money will double in eighteen years. If the rates average 7%, your money will double in a little over ten years.

Table 9.1

Time Period to Double Money

Constant Interest Rate Compounded Semi-Annually	Approximate Number of Years For Investment to Double in Value
3%	24 years
4%	18 years
5%	14.4 years
6%	12 years
7%	10.3 years
8%	9 years
9%	8 years

Table 9.2 shows how much you can expect to save for college by using Savings Bonds in a systematic savings program. Please note that on line one, projections at 4% were guaranteed as a minimum for Bonds purchased March 1993 to April 1995. As you can see from the last column, it will take saving $250 a month for eighteen years at an interest rate of 5% to reach the $86,000 cost projected for four years of college in-state in the first decade of the next century.

Pros and Cons of the Educational Feature

Pros

1. Bonds can be used for the educational expenses of a husband, wife, or children. They are not limited to children only.

2. If not used for education, there is no penalty; you simply are not eligible for federal tax exemption.
3. Bonds can be used at the eligible school of your choice, in-state or out-of-state.
4. There is no set window or time frame for enrollment—anytime after December 31, 1989.
5. You can invest as little as $25 or as much as $15,000 per person per year.
6. The Bonds are backed by the full faith and credit of the U.S. government.
7. The Bonds are no load; there are no commissions or fees for entry or exit.
8. The Bonds are easily purchased through payroll deduction (at participating companies) or from most local banks.

Cons

1. The interest rate may be unattractive to you.
2. The unknown factor of having your tax-free status determined by your income in the year the Bond is redeemed may be too risky. This is especially true if your income is already near the established level and you expect it to outpace inflation.
3. Record keeping is the responsibility of the Bond owner.

An Alternative for Reducing
the Tax Burden

There is an alternative to using Bonds for education with a reduced tax burden. In fact, it may prove to be more of a guarantee than waiting fifteen years to see if your income allows you to qualify for the tax-free status.

You can shift the tax liability to your children by buying the Bonds in their name. The parent can appear as a beneficiary on the Bond, but not as a co-owner. If you register the Bond this way, however, it will not be eligible for the educational feature described earlier.

In choosing this alternative, you must annually report the interest income of the Bonds. If the child's total income is under $600 (this is the limit for 1994; check with IRS for annual adjustments) the child pays no taxes on the interest earned. And because the interest is reported annually, most of it will have been reported by the time the Bonds are redeemed.

To use the annual reporting method, you must file a return the first year to show intent to use this method. You must also file a return any year the child's income exceeds the limit set by the IRS.

Many tax laws change every year, so consult with your accountant before you take any action.

In deciding whether or not to invest in Series EE Savings Bonds for their educational feature, you may want to consider the opinions of others. When reviewing articles please remember that some may have been penned prior to the two latest changes: the guaranteed rate change from 6% to 4%, effective March 1, 1993 to April 30, 1995 and the elimination of the guaranteed rate on new purchases effective May 1, 1995.

Figure 9.1

IRS Form 8815

Form **8815**

Exclusion of Interest From Series EE U.S. Savings Bonds Issued After 1989
(For Filers With Qualified Higher Education Expenses)

OMB No. 1545-1173

1994

Department of the Treasury
Internal Revenue Service

▶ Attach to Form 1040 or Form 1040A.

▶ See instructions on back.

Attachment
Sequence No. **57**

Caution: *If your filing status is married filing a separate return, **do not** file this form. You **cannot** take the exclusion even if you paid qualified higher education expenses in 1994.*

Name(s) shown on return

Your social security number

1	(a) Name of person (you, your spouse, or your dependent) who was enrolled at or attended an eligible educational institution	(b) Name and address of eligible educational institution

If you need more space, attach a statement.

2	Enter the total qualified higher education expenses you paid in 1994 for the persons listed in column (a) of line 1. See the instructions to find out which expenses qualify . . . . . . ▶	2	
3	Enter the total of any nontaxable educational benefits (such as nontaxable scholarship or fellowship grants) received for 1994 for the persons listed in column (a) of line 1. See instructions	3	
4	Subtract line 3 from line 2. If zero or less, **STOP.** You **cannot** take the exclusion	4	
5	Enter the total proceeds (principal and interest) from all series EE U.S. savings bonds **issued after 1989** that you **cashed during 1994**	5	
6	Enter the interest included on line 5. See instructions	6	
7	Is line 4 **less than** line 5? **No.** Enter "1.00." **Yes.** Divide line 4 by line 5. Enter the result as a decimal (to at least two places).	7	× .
8	Multiply line 6 by line 7	8	
9	Enter your modified adjusted gross income. See instructions . . . [9]		
	Note: *If line 9 is $56,200 or more ($91,850 or more if married filing a joint return),* **STOP.** *You **cannot** take the exclusion.*		
10	Enter $41,200 ($61,850 if married filing a joint return) . . . . . [10]		
11	Subtract line 10 from line 9. If zero or less, skip line 12, enter -0- on line 13, and go to line 14 . . . . [11]		
12	Divide line 11 by $15,000 (by $30,000 if married filing a joint return). Enter the result as a decimal (to at least two places)	12	× .
13	Multiply line 8 by line 12	13	
14	**Excludable savings bond interest.** Subtract line 13 from line 8. Enter the result here and on Schedule B (Form 1040), line 3, or Schedule 1 (Form 1040A), line 3, whichever applies . . ▶	14	

Paperwork Reduction Act Notice
We ask for the information on this form to carry out the Internal Revenue laws of the United States. You are required to give us the information. We need it to ensure that you are complying with these laws and to allow us to figure and collect the right amount of tax.

The time needed to complete and file this form will vary depending on individual circumstances. The estimated average time is: **Recordkeeping,** 53 min.; **Learning about the law or the form,** 11 min.; **Preparing the form,** 35 min.; and **Copying, assembling, and sending the form to the IRS,** 34 min.

If you have comments concerning the accuracy of these time estimates or suggestions for making this form more simple, we would be happy to hear from you. You can write to both the IRS and the Office of Management and Budget at the addresses listed in the instructions of the tax return with which this form is filed.

Cat. No. 10822S

Form **8815** (1994)

Figure 9.2

IRS Form 8818

Form 8818
(Rev. July 1992)

Department of the Treasury
Internal Revenue Service

**Optional Form To Record Redemption of Series EE
U.S. Savings Bonds Issued After 1989**
(For Individuals With Qualified Higher Education Expenses)
▶ Keep for your records. **Do not send to the IRS.**
▶ **See instructions on back.**

OMB No. 1545-1151
Expires 4-30-95

Name		Date cashed

1	(a) Serial number	(b) Issue date (must be after 1989)	(c) Face value

2	Add the amounts in column (c) of line 1	2	
3	Total redemption proceeds from bonds listed above that were issued after 1989. Be sure to get this figure from the teller when you cash the bonds	3	
4	Divide line 2 above by 2. This is your cost	4	
5	Subtract line 4 from line 3. This is the interest on the bonds	5	

For Paperwork Reduction Act Notice, see back of form.   Cat. No. 10097L   Form **8818** (Rev. 7-92)

Table 9.2

Using Savings Bonds to Save for Education Expenses

Assumed Interest Rate	Save $50 a month to purchase $300 of Bonds every six months. Value after 10 years.	Save $50 a month to purchase $300 of Bonds every six months. Value after 18 years.	Save $100 a month to purchase $600 of Bonds every six months. Value after 10 years.	Save $100 a month to purchase $600 of Bonds every six months. Value after 18 years.	Save $250 a month to purchase $1500 of Bonds every six months. Value after 10 years.	Save $250 a month to purchase $1500 of Bonds every six months. Value after 18 years.
4%	$7,289	$15,598	$14,578	$31,196	$36,446	$77,991
5%	$7,663	$17,190	$15,326	$34,380	$38,316	$85,952
6%	$8,061	$18,982	$16,122	$37,965	$40,305	$94,913
7%	$8,484	$21,002	$16,968	$42,005	$42,420	$105,011

The calculations in the above table are based the following assumptions:

1. The Bond purchaser will save money at an even monthly rate and will purchase Bonds twice a year. A monthly purchase pattern will result in a slightly higher final value.

2. That the interest rates used to calculate future values will be consistent over the time period the calculations were made.

3. The money invested is the purchase price of the Bonds, not the face value. Thus the term "purchase $300 of Bonds every six months" means $300 purchase price, $600 face value. (Remember EE Bonds are purchased for one-half the face value.)

4. The current guaranteed interest rate for Series EE Bonds purchased March 1, 1993 to April 30, 1995 is 4 percent. Series EE Bonds purchased after April 30, 1995 do not have a guaranteed interest rate (see Chapter 3, New Rules). Call 1-800-USBONDS for interest rate information on new purchases.

Note: This table does not guarantee a specific return on any investment you make. Market conditions and rules governing the Savings Bond program may change without notice. Obtain current rate information and complete details before making any investment.

_____ Chapter 10

EXCHANGING FOR HH BONDS

- ▸ *HH Bonds: What They Are and How They Work*
- ▸ *Points to Consider*
- ▸ *Where to Exchange Bonds and the Process Involved*
- ▸ *Are HH Bonds Right for You?*
- ▸ *Selective Redemption: An Alternative to Exchange*
- ▸ *Tax Consequences of an Exchange*
- ▸ *Timing Your Exchange*
- ▸ *"New Rules" Do Not Impact H/HH Bonds*
- ▸ *Additional Technical Guidelines Covering Exchange*

"To exchange, or not to exchange?" That is the question which plagues many owners of E and EE Bonds. "Should I keep my E and EE Bonds or exchange them for HH?" On the one hand, current income, tax deferral, and direct deposits of interest payments seem very tempting. On the other hand, consider the guaranteed interest rate of only 4% (as of May/1995), with no upside potential for ten years and no tax deferral of the yearly interest income, and the proposition begins to look slightly bleaker.

HH Bonds: What They Are
and How They Work

Series HH Bonds are called "current income Bonds." As the name suggests, these Bonds produce an interest income stream that is paid to the Bond owner every six months. The HH Bond replaced the Series H Bond in January 1980. Many Series H Bonds are still earning interest, although the issuing of new Series H Bonds ended in December 1979.

Series HH Bonds cannot be purchased for cash. They are only available through the exchange of Series E, EE, and Savings Notes. They can also be obtained through the reinvestment of Series H Bonds that have reached final maturity.

HH Bonds come in denominations of $500, $1,000, $5,000, and $10,000. Bond owners must have a minimum redemption value of $500 from any combination of Bonds they are seeking to exchange. Since the HH Bond pays interest every six months, the Bond is always worth the face value upon redemption.

HH Bonds obtained through exchange as of March 1, 1993, will pay a guaranteed interest rate of 4%. The interest is paid semi-annually, direct deposit to the bank account of the Bond holder's choice. This rate is fixed for the first ten years. For the second ten-year period, the Bonds will earn the guaranteed rate that is in effect the day they enter the extended period. The market-based variable rate does not apply to HH Bonds. The total life of the HH Bond is twenty years. See Table 10.2 for interest rates for H and HH Bonds.

All H and HH Bonds that are still paying interest have an initial maturity of ten years. H Bonds receive two ten-year extensions for a total life of thirty years. HH Bonds receive one ten-year extension for a total life of twenty years. Many Bond owners are surprised (and disappointed) that the Bonds pick up the current guaranteed rate in effect each time a new ten-year extension is started. This new rate is in effect for that ten-year period. Retirees on fixed incomes, who originally exchanged for Bonds in the mid-1980s at 7.5%, have been upset to find that the semi-annual interest payment they are used to is cut almost in half (to 4%) as their HH Bonds enter into a ten-year extension in the mid-1990s. See Table 10.2 for interest rates for Series H and HH Bonds.

Points to Consider

You only have to hold your Series E and EE Bonds and Savings Notes for six months before they are eligible to exchange for HH Bonds. At final maturity (i.e., the date the Bond stops earning interest) the Bond owner has one year to exchange those Bonds for HH Bonds. After the Bonds are one year past final maturity they are no longer eligible for exchange.

You may defer reporting interest earned on Series E, EE, and Savings Notes until the HH Bonds received in exchange are redeemed, disposed of (for example, taxable reissue), or have reached final maturity, whichever comes first. The deferred interest will be reported to the Bond owner and to the IRS at the time the HH Bonds reach such a taxable event. Since HH Bonds have a total life of twenty years, Bond owners can receive up to twenty years of additional tax deferral when they exchange to HH Bonds.

The semi-annual interest payments from the HH Bonds must be reported as interest income. This interest is subject to federal income taxes, but exempt from state and local taxes.

Unlike Series EE Bonds which have a purchase limit, you may exchange for an unlimited dollar amount of HH Bonds. (Refer to Chapter 12, "Purchasing U.S. Savings Bonds," for additional information on purchase limits.)

If you exchange a substantial dollar amount, consider requesting smaller denominations of HH Bonds such as $500 or $1,000 denominations instead of $10,000 denominations. Why? At a later date if you want to cash in a few thousand dollars here or there, you can select the exact number of Bonds you need for your redemption needs. You can in fact cash in part of a $10,000 Bond and have the remainder reissued; however, this requires more paperwork.

Where to Exchange Bonds and the Process Involved

The process of exchanging other Bonds for HH Bonds is simply transferring the value of those Bonds into HH Bonds. The transaction can be handled at most commercial banks. If your bank handles the redemption of Savings Bonds, they should be familiar with the exchange procedure.

The form to use for exchanging is PD F 3253 (Figure 10.1). The bank will record the redemption value of the Bonds you present for exchange on the PD F 3253. (If you want to double check their calculations, see Chapter 6 for options.) The value of the Bonds you present for exchange will probably not exactly match the $500 increments of HH Bonds. You may add money to the transaction, up to the next $500 increment, or you may take money back, down to the next $500 increment. This is your choice—do not let the bank teller make it for you. If you choose to receive money, thus rounding down to the nearest

$500 denomination of HH Bond, some or all of the money you receive is interest from the old Bonds. The amount of interest will be reported as interest income for the year in which the exchange takes place.

The PD F 3253 includes an authorization for direct deposit of the interest payments to an account at the financial institution of your choice. The direct deposit feature has been required for all HH Bonds issued since October 1989.

Are HH Bonds Right for You?

When might HH Bonds be a good investment for you? They might be attractive when you have money in a savings account paying only 2% to 3% or when you could use the semi-annual interest payments to supplement your income.

If you have at least $500, and can afford to tie it up for one year, this HH Bond scenario might work. Buy an EE Bond for $500 ($1,000 face value). Hold the Bond for six months and then exchange it for an HH Bond. At the time of exchange, you can receive the interest you earned on the EE Bond. Once you have held the HH Bond six months, your semi-annual payment will be direct deposited to your bank account. If you are only earning 2% on your savings account, this is a quick way to double your earnings. You can cash the HH Bond anytime after holding it six months.

Another option Bond Owners use, is to exchange at final maturity if they need another one or two years of deferral before they want to report the interest income. By exchanging, the Bond owner now has up to twenty years in which to time the redemption to suit their specific situation.

When are HH Bonds *not* a good idea? In a *Newsweek* piece dated July 4, 1994, Jane Bryant Quinn tackles a Savings Bond exchange question by presenting Treasury Notes as her preferred choice. This article should be read by any Bond owner considering an exchange at final maturity.

To summarize, each Bond owner's situation is unique. A case can be made for or against HH Bonds, depending on the variables of each individual's situation.

Selective Redemption:
An Alternative to Exchange

Smart Bond owners take time to study their options. The information presented in this section is intended to provide you with a system that will maximize the return on your Savings Bond investment.

If you own U.S. Savings Bonds, at some point you will be cashing them or exchanging them for HH Bonds. Given the changes in the guaranteed interest rate implemented by the government in March 1993, it is important to understand the consequences of redeeming or exchanging Bonds.

Millions of Americans bought Savings Bonds with the intent of exchanging them for HH Bonds to supplement their retirement income. This strategy was more attractive when HH Bonds paid 6%; on March 1, 1993, however, as a result of the drop in the interest rate, HH Bonds began paying only 4%. Here is what most Bond owners fail to realize:

1. Many of their E and EE Bonds may still have a guaranteed rate of 6% or 7.5%. Exchanging would result in forfeiting 2 to 3.5 interest points on many Bonds. A drop in the interest rate of 3.5% results in lost interest of $350 per $10,000.

2. When you exchange during the 4% rate period that was enacted March 1, 1993, the 4% rate is locked for ten years. Even if rates increase after you exchanged, you will remain at 4% for the first ten years. You can cash your HH Bond after six months; however, you then have to report any interest that was deferred from the E or EE Bonds when you exchanged—which is probably what prompted you to exchange in the first place.

What is selective redemption? Selective redemption is a process wherein the Bond owner chooses which Bonds to redeem or exchange based on interest rates and timing issues. When Bonds need to be cashed or redeemed, the goal is to divest the lower-paying interest Bonds and hold on to those earning higher rates. Selective redemption is *not* grabbing a handful of Bonds and redeeming or exchanging with no forethought.

How does it work? Let's suppose you were going to exchange your Bonds for HH Bonds. To use selective redemption instead of exchanging, you would cash Bonds that would equal the dollar amount you would have received in interest had you exchanged for HH Bonds. This allows you to keep the majority of your E and EE Bonds at the higher rates of interest. When selecting which E and EE Bonds to cash, choose those that are earning the lowest rate of interest.

One advantage of this strategy is that it puts off the exchange decision for an indefinite period of time. Thus, if rates on Savings Bonds are increased in 1996 or 1997, you could then exchange for HH Bonds at the new higher rate. This would mean you lock in the new higher rate for the next ten years.

Consider this example. A Bond owner has Series E Bonds with a redemption value of $10,000. If he exchanges the E Bonds for HH Bonds, he will receive one $10,000 HH Bond that is paying 4%. The annual interest earned on that Bond is $400. The entire $400 will be reported as interest income for tax purposes.

Instead of exchanging his Bonds, this Bond owner uses the selective redemption system. First he determines the exact interest rate that applies to each of his Bonds. He learns that some of his Bonds are earning 4%, some 6%, and some 7.5%. On average he is earning about 5.8% on his Series E Bonds. After identifying the Bonds earning 4%, he decides to cash a few of the them, receiving approximately $400.

What is the result? A comparison at the end of one year is illustrated in Table 10.1.

Table 10.1

Comparison of Exchange and Selective Redemption

AFTER ONE YEAR...	EXCHANGING FOR HH BONDS	SELECTIVE REDEMPTION
Value of remaining Bonds:	$10,000	Approximately $10,180
Proceeds:	$400 from interest payments	$400 from redemption
Tax consequence:	All $400 is interest income	$400 minus original purchase price of E Bonds is interest income
Future options:	Locked in 4% for ten years, have to cash HH Bonds if you want to exercise other options.	Can continue selective redemption for an indefinite period, or can exchange to HH Bonds at any time if HH Bond rate is increased to more attractive level. Keeps options open.

In this example, selective redemption resulted in an even flow of dollars (redemption proceeds) to the Bond owner and an increase in the Bond holdings of $180. The actual numbers will vary in each case. The primary numbers that may make this option attractive are the interest rates on the E and EE Bonds. If those guaranteed rates are at 6.0% or 7.5%, then selective redemption makes a lot of sense.

To effectively use this strategy, you need to know the exact interest rates, values, and timing issues for each Bond you own. Chapter 6 outlines the options for obtaining this information for your Bonds.

If a Bond has reached final maturity, your only option is to redeem or exchange it (if the Bond is less than one year past final maturity).

Tax Consequences of an Exchange

Because most Bond owners do not report the interest accruing on their E and EE Bonds annually, they must report it when the Bonds are redeemed. When exchanging for HH Bonds, the Bond owner has the options of (a) reporting all interest accrued for the Bonds presented for exchange or (b) deferring the reporting of the interest until the HH Bond is cashed, reaches final maturity, or is disposed of in a manner that creates a taxable event. By electing to defer the interest reporting, the Bond owner may receive up to twenty years of additional deferral (the life of the HH Bond is twenty years).

The option of whether to report or defer accrued interest is the Bond owner's choice. If a bank teller is assisting you, advise him or her of your choice. Do not allow anyone to assign you an option without your consent.

How to Know the Amount of Deferred Interest

If you choose to defer the accrued interest from the Bonds you are exchanging, the amount deferred will be printed on the face of your HH Bonds.

For example, a Bond owner exchanges $20,000 (redemption value) of Series E Bonds for Series HH Bonds. Of that $20,000, the purchase price was $6,000 and the interest accrued $14,000. The Bond owner receives two $10,000 HH Bonds. On the face of each HH Bond is a statement similar to the following:

> Deferred interest $7,000 on Savings Bonds/Savings Notes exchanged for this Bond and included in its issue price is reportable for federal income tax purposes, for the year of redemption, disposition, or final maturity of this Bond, which ever is earlier.

The $7,000 mentioned on the two Bonds adds up to the $14,000 of accrued and deferred interest. When the Bond owner redeems the HH Bonds, he will receive $20,000 and a 1099-INT for $14,000 in interest income.

Timing Your Exchange

The more you can get from your E and EE Bonds and SNs, the more you have to invest in HH Bonds. Since most E and EE Bonds and SNs increase in value semi-annually, exchanging right after a semi-annual increase will maximize the amount available for exchange. Tables 6.5 and 6.6 provide the date of increase for your E and EE Bonds.

You will receive an interest payment the month of exchange and another six months later. If you exchanged in January, your interest payment will come every July and January. Thus, if you want payments twice a year, transact all your exchanges in the same month. (More than likely this will not maximize the timing on the Bonds being presented for exchange.) Or if you prefer to receive an interest payment every month, spread your exchange requests over a consecutive six-month period. This will insure that you receive an interest payment all twelve months of the year.

"New Rules" Do Not Impact H/HH Bonds

The new rules that were implemented May 1, 1995, do not affect any new or old issues of H or HH Bonds. H/HH Bonds have never been impacted by the market-based rates and this is still the case.

Under the current rules that apply to H/HH Bonds, any future announcements of a change in the guaranteed interest rates would impact H/HH Bonds as they entered extended maturity periods. For more information on extended maturity periods, see Chapter 4.

Additional Technical Guidelines
Covering Exchange

The remainder of this chapter is fairly technical; if you have had your fill, move on to the next chapter. If you want more details, indulge yourself. The information in this section, some of which has been adapted for your benefit, is from The Department of Treasury, The Bureau of the Public Debt's (BPD) publication, "The Book on U.S. Savings Bonds."

There are some situations where Bond owners have reported the interest on their Bonds and Savings Notes annually. These Bonds and Savings Notes may be exchanged for Series HH Bonds also.

When further deferral of the tax liability is elected in the exchange, the rules on registration of the Bonds are as follows:

1. If the accrual Bonds and Savings Notes are registered in single ownership or beneficiary form, the person named as owner must also be named as owner or first-named co-owner on the HH Bonds.

   A beneficiary may be added, changed, or removed or a co-owner may be added to the registration.

2. If the accrual-type Bonds and Savings Notes are registered in co-ownership form, the "principal co-owner" (the one whose funds were used to purchase the Bonds and Savings Notes) must be named as owner or first-named co-owner on the HH Bonds. The other co-owner could be changed or removed or a beneficiary added. If both co-owners shared equally in the purchase or received them jointly as gifts of a legacy, the registration on the Series HH Bond must name both persons as co-owners.

3. If the owner or "principal co-owner" of the older Bonds and Savings Notes is deceased, and there is a surviving beneficiary or co-owner, the latter must be named as owner or first-named co-owner on the HH Bonds. The person submitting the Bonds and Savings Notes for exchange must submit evidence establishing entitlement (for example, the beneficiary must furnish proof of death of the registered owner). Another co-owner or beneficiary could be named.

Advice on how to resolve difficult situations can be obtained from the BPD. (See Chapter 17 for address and phone number.)

Who May Request Exchange and Changes in Registration

The Owner. The term "owner" means: (1) the registered owner of a security registered in single ownership or beneficiary form, whether or not a natural person, or (2) a beneficiary or co-owner named on a security with a deceased owner or co-owner. The beneficiary would be required to furnish proof of the owner's death. An owner may request the exchange and have the HH Bonds issued in his or her name in any authorized form of registration permitted under Department of the Treasury Circular, Public Debt Series 3-80, provided he or she is owner or first-named co-owner.

The Co-owner. A "principal co-owner" is one who (1) purchased the securities with his or her own funds or (2) received them as a gift, legacy, or inheritance, or as a result of judicial proceedings, and had them reissued in co-ownership form, provided he or she received no contribution in any manner from the other co-owner for being so designated. (Those processing the exchange subscription form PD F 3253 are not required to go beyond a person's certification on such form that he or she is the principal co-owner of the securities presented.)

The principal co-owner of the securities presented for exchange must be named as owner or first-named co-owner on the Series HH Bonds and his or her Social Security number must be provided.

Co-owners Who May Request An Exchange

Either co-owner may request the exchange, that is, if there is no change in registration and the HH Bond is to be registered exactly the same way the securities surrendered had been.

If a tax-deferred exchange is requested, the Social Security account number of the "principal co-owner" (whose name must be shown first in the inscription) must be used for Bonds to be inscribed in the names of two persons as co-owners.

If the principal co-owner is not the person requesting the exchange, the principal co-owner must complete Form W-9 to certify the correctness of his or her Social Security account number and that he or she is not subject to backup withholding. In such cases, the co-owner requesting the exchange must also strike the statement on PD F 3253 above his or her signature that he or she is the principal co-owner.

Only the principal co-owner may request an exchange if the HH Bonds are to be registered differently from the securities surrendered. Such HH Bond registration may be in any form permitted by Department of the Treasury Circular, Public Debt Series 3-80, but must include the principal co-owner as the owner or first-named co-owner.

Legal Representative (Named in Registration on the Bond)

A legal representative means the court-appointed (or otherwise qualified) person, regardless of title, who is legally authorized to act for the estate of a minor, incompetent, aged person, absentee, et al. The legal representative would be required to show full title and provide appropriate identification. Legal representatives of decedents' estates should not conduct exchanges but should request distribution on PD F 1455 so that persons entitled to the estate may do so.

More Than One Form of Inscription Requested

Subject to the limitations stated above, a subscriber may request that the HH Bonds be issued in several inscriptions. A note to that effect should be made on the face of the form with the additional inscriptions recorded, together with the appropriate amounts for each, on the back of the blue (A) copy of Form PD F 3253. The person authorized to request the exchange must execute the requests for payment on the Bonds.

To sum it up, HH Bonds can be valuable if you have specific financial goals in mind. Knowing your options will help you determine the wisest investment of your Savings Bond dollars. "To exchange, or not to exchange?" Only you can answer that!

Figure 10.1
Exchange Application (PD F 3253)

PD F 3253
Department of the Treasury
Bureau of the Public Debt
(Revised March 1990)

OMB No. 1535-0005
Expires 9/30/91

EXCHANGE APPLICATION FOR U.S. SAVINGS BONDS OF SERIES HH
Please follow the attached instructions and use worksheet when completing the form

1. For Federal income tax purposes, I   (a) wish to defer reporting   (b) will report this year or have reported the interest earned on my bonds/notes surrendered in this exchange transaction.

2. $.	3. $.	4. $.	5. $.	6. $.
Redemption Value	Interest Earned	HH Bonds To Be Issued	Payment Returned	Interest Deferred

7. Number Of Each Denomination		$500		$1,000		$5,000		$10,000
FRB USE	Increment On Each Bond							
ONLY	Bond Serial Numbers							

8. REGISTRATION INFORMATION

OWNER OR FIRST-NAMED COOWNER (Bonds registered to)

TAXPAYER
IDENTIFICATION NO.:   —   —   -- OR --   —

Social Security Number   Employer Identification Number

NAME:

NUMBER AND STREET
OR RURAL ROUTE:

CITY / TOWN: STATE: ZIP CODE:

COOWNER OR BENEFICIARY (OPTIONAL). **Coownership will be assumed if neither block is checked.** The following person is to be named as   coowner   beneficiary.   See reverse for additional registrations.

NAME:

Delivery Instructions for HH
bonds (if different than above): _____

9. DIRECT DEPOSIT AUTHORIZATION (Read instructions before completing this section).

NAME(S) ON
DEPOSITOR ACCT.: _____

ROUTING/
TRANSIT NO.: _____

DEPOSITOR
ACCT. NO.:

TYPE OF ACCOUNT: CHECKING   SAVINGS

I request that semiannual interest payments on Series HH/H bonds purchased prior to October 1989 and bearing the above taxpayer identification number also be deposited directly to this account. **If neither block is checked, yes will be assumed.**   YES   NO

10. Under penalty of perjury, I certify that I am the owner or principal coowner of any savings bonds and notes submitted herewith; that the number shown on the form is my correct taxpayer identification number; and that I am not subject to backup withholding either (i) because I have not been notified that I am subject to backup withholding (as a result of a failure to report all interest and dividends) or (ii) because I have been notified by the Internal Revenue Service that I am no longer subject to backup withholding, unless I check this block: ☐ I am subject to backup withholding.

Daytime
Telephone No.: _____   Serial Number of one savings bond/note surrendered in this exchange: _____

Applicant's Signature: _____   Date _____

11. FINANCIAL INSTITUTION AUTHORIZATION AND CERTIFICATION

NAME, ADDRESS, AND TELEPHONE NO.:

As representative of the financial institution named in this Item, I certify that the account name(s) and number shown in Item 9 are correct and that the financial institution agrees to receive and deposit the semiannual interest payments on the Series HH bonds issued pursuant to this form in accordance with applicable regulations.

PAYMENT METHOD:
☐ Charge Reserve Account *   ☐ Check

*ABA NUMBER: _____

Payment Stamp

(Authorized Signature)   (Date)

FRB USE ONLY   CASE NO.:   A. Federal Reserve Bank Copy

Table 10.2

Interest Rates For Series HH and H Bonds

(Valid for June 1995 only)

Issue Date	Original Maturity Period	Guaranteed Through Current Maturity Period	Date Next Extension Begins	Life of Bond
SERIES HH				
March 1993 to ...	10 years	4.0	March 2003 to ...	20 years
November 1986 to February 1993	10 years	6.0	November 1996 to February 2003	20 years
June 1985 to October 1986	10 years	7.5	June 1995 to October 1996	20 years
March 1983 to May 1985	10 years	4.0	currently in final extension	20 years
January 1980 to February 1983	10 years	6.0	currently in final extension	20 years
SERIES H				
November 1976 to December 1979	10 years	6.0	November 1996 to December 1999	30 years
June 1975 to October 1976	10 years	7.5	June 1995 to October 1996	30 years
March 1973 to May 1975	10 years	4.0	currently in final extension	30 years
November 1966 to February 1973	10 years	6.0	currently in final extension	30 years
July 1965 to October 1966	10 years	7.5	currently in final extension	30 years
June 1952 to June 1965	N/A	0.0	Bonds reached final maturity	30 years

Adapted from Department of Treasury, Bureau of the Public Debt, U.S. Savings Bond Marketing Office.

Chapter 11

REISSUING U.S. SAVINGS BONDS

- ▸ *Common Reissue Cases*
- ▸ *When Bonds Do Not Need to Be Reissued*
- ▸ *How to Reissue Bonds*
- ▸ *Who Can Help with the Forms: Cost for Assistance*
- ▸ *Which Reissue Transactions Create a Taxable Event*
- ▸ *What Reissue Forms Are Available and from Where*
- ▸ *Where to Send the Reissue Forms*

"Reissue" is the term used by The Federal Reserve Banks (FRB) and The Bureau of the Public Debt (BPD) to describe the change of a registration on a U.S. Savings Bond. The public often uses the word "retitled."

There are literally hundreds of variables that can impact any given reissue case. This chapter will attempt to deal with some of the most common cases and questions, as well as present resources available to the Bond owner.

As you will see in the following story, knowing your reissue options is vital to managing your Bond investment.

The year was 1992, the state, Arkansas—and no, this story is not about a presidential election. A wife and mother had just suffered the loss of her husband. They had been married for several decades.

Over the years they had purchased a stack of U.S. Savings Bonds worth over $200,000. Both of their names were on the Bonds as co-owners. After several months, she began to attend to her financial matters and, in the process, took the Bonds to her bank to ask what she should do. After listening to her situation, the bank representative told her she "must redeem the Bonds."

Cashing the Bonds would mean having to report $150,000 of interest income, with a minimum tax bite of over $50,000. Fortunately, this woman sought a second opinion and received an answer that was totally different from what the bank had told her.

A written analysis of this woman's Bonds from The Savings Bond Informer, Inc., revealed that they all had over eight years of interest-earning life left. She was listed as a co-owner on the Bonds and in *no way* did she have to redeem them. She could simply have them reissued. This means that she would have her deceased husband's name removed and her name put first, adding the co-owner or beneficiary of her choice. Reissuing, in this case, is not a taxable event. Once the Bonds are reissued she could hold them to final maturity, exchange them for HH Bonds and continue the tax deferral, or selectively redeem them over a period of years to spread the tax liability.

When appropriate, reissuing Savings Bonds can often provide advantageous financial and/or timing options to the Bond owner. When seeking answers to reissue questions, never take the verbal advice of anyone without confirming what they say with the FRB or the BPD (see Chapter 17 for phone numbers and addresses).

Common Reissue Cases

There are hundreds of reasons why a Bond might need to be reissued. Here are some of the most common:

✓ To add a co-owner or beneficiary to a Bond that is presently in one name only (See Figure 11.1, PD F 4000)

✓ To change the beneficiary that is presently listed on the Bond to co-owner (See Figure 11.1, PD F 4000)

✓ To correct an error in the way the Bond was inscribed by the issuing agent

✓ To eliminate the name of a deceased co-owner or beneficiary and add another person in his/her place (See Figure 11.1, PD F 4000)

✓ To have the Bonds retitled into a trust (See Figure 11.2, PD F 1851

✓ To remove the name of a living person from the Bond (Note: This may create a taxable event and may require the consent of the party being removed.)

When Bonds Do Not Need to Be Reissued

U.S. Savings Bonds do not need to be reissued for the following cases.

1. The government will not reissue Series E and EE Bonds or Savings Notes for a change of address. The average American moves five to eight times over a thirty- to forty-year period. Your address has no bearing on your Bond. **Note:** Owners of Series H and HH Bonds are required to notify the Bureau of the Public Debt so that interest account records can be updated. Current addresses are needed to deliver the forms 1099-INT to these Bond owners.

2. A Savings Bond does not need to be reissued for a change of name due to marriage. The Bond may still be redeemed with proper identification. The person named on the Bond will sign her married name, "changed by marriage from," and then sign her maiden name.

How to Reissue Bonds

This section will briefly examine the steps you must complete to have your Savings Bonds reissued. If you choose to have a professional handle your transaction, you can let him or her worry about these steps.

1. Identify and order the proper reissue form. One of the FRB regional sites or the BPD can assist you. A brief description of each form is given later in this chapter.

2. Read the instructions that come with each form. They are in small print, but hang in there. The instructions will address most of your questions.

3. Complete the form in full. The author suggests working on the form on a weekday during normal business hours, if possible. Then, if you have a question or quandary, a phone call to the BPD or your regional FRB can be made immediately. (They do not staff their phones on the weekends or in the evenings.) Be prepared for a lengthy process; most forms require listing serial numbers, issue dates, face values and registration information for each Bond.

4. Secure the necessary signature guarantees, certifications, or notarizations.

5. Once you are satisfied that you have completed the form properly, make a photocopy for your own records.

6. Send the form, the Bonds, and any additional paperwork required to the FRB or take the bundle to your bank and ask that they forward it for you. See "Where to Send the Reissue Forms" later in this chapter.

Special note: For most reissue transactions, you will *not* need to sign the Bonds. In all cases, however, the appropriate person(s) must sign the form and their signatures must be either certified, guaranteed, or notarized.

Who Can Help with the Forms:
Cost for Assistance

The Bond owner has several avenues for assistance when completing reissue forms. In the "do-it-yourself" scenario, a Bond owner can call the appropriate regional FRB site or the BPD. They will answer your questions but it will be your responsibility to enter the correct information onto the appropriate reissue form. There is no cost for this assistance.

If you would prefer to have someone else complete the paperwork for you, here are several other options.

Commercial Banks. Many banks will complete reissue forms for Bond owners. The cost will vary from bank to bank because banks are free to create their own policies regarding what work they will do and how much they will charge. Many banks will not charge a fee to complete the reissue forms, although this may be limited to customers of the bank. Other banks will charge as much as $2 a Bond: $400 if you have 200 Bonds. Ask for a quote in writing before you let them begin. Caution: If your bank seldom completes reissue forms, they may not be the best choice. If they frequently process reissue requests and there is no charge, that could be a winning combination.

Financial Professionals. With the increase in personal trusts and total financial planning, many people in the financial professional community provide assistance on reissue forms. As with the banks, price and level of service will vary. If you choose a financial professional (attorney, accountant, financial planner, or bank representative) to handle your reissue transaction, ask for a price quote in writing. If they are familiar with Bonds, they should be able to estimate the time this task will take and provide a quote.

Which Reissue Transactions Create a Taxable Event

Certain types of reissue transactions generate a taxable event for the Bond owner. A detailed review of which transactions create taxable events is covered in Chapter 8, "Taxation Issues for U.S. Savings Bonds."

One question appears with regularity among Bond owner reissue inquiries: "I am on these Savings Bonds, and I would like to remove my name and give the Bonds to my grandchildren. Can I do that?" Yes, you can, but do you want to? The case just described will create a taxable event for Grandpa. If he removes his name, he will have to report all the interest earned on the Bonds up to that point in time, even though he will receive no money from the Bonds.

Even worse is that when a grandchild cashes a Bond ten or twenty years later, he or she will receive a 1099-INT for all the interest it ever earned. If they do not know that some of the interest had been reported by Grandpa, they will report all the interest themselves. Thus, part of the interest will be taxed twice (see Chapter 8, "Watch Out for Double Taxation"). When reporting interest income from U.S. Savings Bonds, the specific Bonds and serial numbers are not listed on the 1099-INT. The IRS has no easy way of knowing or tracking the fact that interest on a particular Bond may have been reported twice.

Removing the principal co-owner (normally considered the first-named party, unless evidence can be produced to show otherwise) from a Bond while that person is still living creates a taxable event for the principal co-owner.

For reissue transactions that create taxable events, the FRB requires that you complete an additional form stating that you are aware that this transaction will generate a 1099-INT.

What Reissue Forms Are Available
and from Where

The following list of Public Debt (PD) forms are available from the five regional FRBs and from the BPD (listed in Chapter 17). Commercial banks may carry some of the forms, particularly the ones that are requested most often.

PD F 1455
Request by Fiduciary for Reissue of United States Savings Bonds/ Notes

PD F 1851
Request for Reissue of United States Savings Bonds/Notes in Name of Trustee of Personal Trust Estate

PD F 1938
Request for Reissue of United States Savings Bonds/Notes During the Lives of Both Co-owners

PD F 1946
Application for Disposition—United States Savings Bonds/Notes and/or Related Checks (in a Combined Amount Not Exceeding $1,000) Owned by Decedent Whose Estate is Being Settled Without Administration

PD F 1946-1
Application for Disposition—United States Savings Bonds/Notes and/or Related Checks Owned by Decedent Whose Estate is Being Settled Without Administration.

PD F 3360
Request for Reissue of United States Savings Bonds/Notes in the Name of a Person or Persons Other Than the Owner (Including Legal Guardian, Custodian for a Minor Under a Statute, etc.)

PD F 4000
Request by Owner for Reissue of United States Savings Bonds/Notes to Add Beneficiary or Co-owner, Eliminate Beneficiary or Decedent, Show Change of Name, and/or Correct Error in Registration

Where to Send the
Reissue Forms

All reissue transactions are processed by a regional FRB or the BPD. You may submit your transaction to your local commercial bank for forwarding or you may mail directly to the appropriate regional FRB processing site. (See Chapter 17 for address and phone number.)

If your commercial bank is an authorized issuing and paying agent (that means they sell and redeem Bonds), they will probably be familiar with the appropriate regional FRB site and thus be willing to forward your transaction. The advantages of this is that you will save postage and should there be a problem the bank can verify that the transaction was submitted. The disadvantage is that, in some cases, it may take a little longer to travel through the bank's mailing or delivery system.

The second option is to submit your transaction directly to the appropriate FRB regional processing site. If you choose this option, it is best to send your transaction by registered or certified mail, return receipt requested. The receipt becomes important in case there is any problem locating the transaction. The receipt will verify whether it reached the FRB or not. Should special handling or rulings be required for a particular reissue case, the FRB may forward the case to the BPD.

Unfortunately, the need to reissue Bonds can come at a time that is less than ideal, that is, after the death of a loved one. If you follow the suggestions in this chapter and are patient in pursuing the correct avenues of assistance, reissuing Bonds can be a relatively easy, although time-intensive, process.

Figure 11.1

Reissue Form PD F 4000

PD F 4000
Department of the Treasury
Bureau of the Public Debt
(Revised May 1989)

REQUEST BY OWNER FOR REISSUE OF UNITED STATES
SAVINGS BONDS/NOTES TO ADD BENEFICIARY OR COOWNER,
ELIMINATE BENEFICIARY OR DECEDENT, SHOW CHANGE
OF NAME, AND/OR CORRECT ERROR IN REGISTRATION

OMB No. 1535-0023

IMPORTANT: Follow instructions on the reverse in filling out this form. Any person who makes a statement on this form knowing it to be false, fictitious or fraudulent may be fined $10,000 or imprisoned for five years, or both.
PRINT IN INK OR TYPE ALL INFORMATION.

PAPERWORK REDUCTION STATEMENT: The completion of this form by any member of the public is voluntary. However, if completion of the transaction named below is desired, the information on this form must be provided.

To: Federal Reserve Bank

The undersigned hereby presents and surrenders for reissue the following-described United States Savings Bonds.

Total face amount _____

ISSUE DATE	DENOMINATION (FACE AMOUNT)	SERIAL NUMBER	INSCRIPTION (Please type or print names, including middle names or initials, social security account number, if any, and addresses as inscribed on the bonds.)

(If space is insufficient use continuation sheet on page 4, sign it and refer to it above -- or use Form PD 3500 for this purpose.)

I hereby certify that _____ is the principal coowner of any bonds registered in coownership form
(Name of coowner)

submitted herewith and is responsible for any federal tax liability arising from this transaction (SEE TAX LIABILITY NOTICE), and I hereby request that said bonds be reissued in the following form of registration:

Mr. ☐   Mrs. ☐   Miss ☐ _____

(First name)   (Middle name or initial)   (Last name)

Address _____

(Number and street or rural route)   (City or town)   (State)   (ZIP Code)

If a coowner or beneficiary is desired, complete the following line:

With Mr. ☐   Mrs. ☐   Miss ☐ _____ as { ☐ coowner
                                                         ☐ beneficiary

(First name)   (Middle name or initial)   (Last name)

TAXPAYER IDENTIFYING NUMBERS (See General Instructions, page 3)

☐☐☐ – ☐☐ – ☐☐☐☐   ☐☐☐ – ☐☐ – ☐☐☐☐   ☐☐ – ☐☐☐☐☐☐☐

(S.S. No. - Owner or first coowner)   (S.S. No. - Second coowner or beneficiary)   (Employer Identification Number)

If new bonds are not to be delivered to address shown thereon, give delivery instructions here.

Name _____
Address _____

(Number and street or rural route)   (City or town)   (State)   (ZIP Code)

Reissue is requested for the reason(s) shown below:

```
IN ALL CASES
THIS FORM MUST BE SIGNED
ON THE REVERSE SIDE
```

1. ☐ To add a coowner or beneficiary.
2. ☐ To change present beneficiary to coowner.
3. ☐ To eliminate a living beneficiary and reissue the bonds in either single ownership form or with another person as coowner or beneficiary. (For Series E and H bonds and savings notes, the present beneficiary must consent on page 2.)
4. ☐ To reissue in the name of a surviving owner, coowner, or beneficiary or in his/her name and that of another person as coowner or beneficiary. (Proof of death of owner, coowner, or beneficiary named on Series E or H bonds or savings notes, and owner or coowner named on Series EE or HH bonds, must be furnished.)
5. ☐ Change of name by: (a) ☐ marriage   (b) ☐ divorce   (c) ☐ court order   (d) ☐ naturalization   (e) ☐ otherwise   if (e) is checked, furnish explanation: _____
6. ☐ Correct error in registration. (See specific instruction No. 6) Provide following information:
   (a) The bonds were purchased by: _____
   (b) The funds belonged to: _____
   (c) Explanation of error _____

Figure 11.2

Reissue Form PD F 1851

REQUEST FOR REISSUE OF UNITED STATES SAVINGS BONDS/NOTES
IN NAME OF TRUSTEE OF PERSONAL TRUST ESTATE

PD F 1851
Department of the Treasury
Bureau of the Public Debt
(Revised April 1990)

IMPORTANT - Before filling out form, read instructions INCLUDING TAX LIABILITY NOTICE. Any person who makes a claim or statement on this form knowing it to be false, fictitious, or fraudulent may be fined $10,000 or imprisoned for 5 years, or both.
PRINT IN INK OR TYPE ALL INFORMATION.

TO: Federal Reserve Bank

BEFORE FILLING OUT THIS FORM, READ TAX LIABILITY NOTICE ON PAGE 3
(The applicable statement(s) below MUST be completed; see instructions.)

1. I (we) hereby request reissue of the bonds described on the reverse hereof in the form set out in item 5 below to the extent of

   $_____ (face amount).

2. In support of this request, I (we severally) certify that the trust estate described in item 5 below is a personal trust estate as defined in item 1 of the instructions on page 3 of this form, and

   a. [ ] was created by _____
   (Name(s) of owner or both coowners creating trust)

   b. [ ] was created by one coowner, _____
   (Name of coowner creating trust)

   c. [ ] was created by some other person and
   (i) [ ] I am (one of us is) a beneficiary of the trust.   [ ][ ][ ] – [ ][ ] – [ ][ ][ ][ ]

   (ii) [ ] _____, a beneficiary of the trust, is related
   (Name)

   to_____ as_____
   (Name of owner or coowner)   (Give exact relationship)

3. You must check box a. or b. (SEE "TAX LIABILITY" SECTION OF INSTRUCTIONS):

   a. [ ] I (we) certify that, for federal income tax purposes, I (we) will be treated as owner(s) of the portion of the trust represented by any tax-deferred accumulated interest on the surrendered bonds.

   b. [ ] I (we) certify that, for federal income tax purposes, I (we) will not be treated as owner(s) of the portion of the trust represented by any tax-deferred accumulated interest on the surrendered bonds, and therefore, I (we) will include the tax-deferred accumulated interest in gross income for the taxable year in which the bonds are reissued to the trust. I (we) am aware that a 1099 INT will be issued and the interest will be reported to the Internal Revenue Service by the agent that processes the transaction. The interest which will be reported includes deferred interest on H/HH bonds as well as interest earned on E/EE bonds from the issue date until the date of reissue.

4. _____ is the principal coowner of any bonds registered in coownership
   (Name of coowner)

   form submitted herewith. (A principal coowner is a coowner who (1) purchased the bonds with his or her own funds or (2) received them as a gift, inheritance or legacy, or as a result of judicial proceedings, and has them reissued in coownership form, provided he or she has received no contribution in money or money's worth for designating the other coowner on the bonds.) The above-named principal coowners is responsible for any tax liability arising from the reissue transaction requested hereon and his/her Social Security Account Number is:

   [ ][ ][ ] – [ ][ ] – [ ][ ][ ][ ]

   (Failure to furnish this information could cause rejection of the transaction.)

5. Form in which bonds _____
   are to be reissued.   (Inscription: include name(s) of trustee(s), name(s) of creator(s) or trustor(s) and date of trust's creation)

   _____
   (Address)

   (Taxpayer Identifying
   Number Assigned to   [ ][ ] [ ][ ][ ][ ][ ][ ][ ]   [ ][ ][ ] – [ ][ ] – [ ][ ][ ][ ]
   Trust)   (Employer Identification Number)   (Social Security Account Number)

   If the new bonds are not to be   _____
   delivered to address shown   (Name)
   thereon deliver them to: _____
                                       (Street Address)

   _____
   (City or town)   (State)   (Zip Code)

OWNER AND OTHER REGISTRANTS MUST SIGN AND HAVE THEIR SIGNATURES CERTIFIED ON PAGE 2

(1)

_____ Chapter 12

PURCHASING U.S. SAVINGS BONDS

- ► *An Explanation of Bonds Available Today*
- ► *When Is the Best Time to Purchase Bonds?*
- ► *Where and How Can Bonds Be Purchased?*
- ► *Who Can Buy U.S. Savings Bonds?*
- ► *Purchase Limitations*
- ► *How to Compute whose Purchase Limit is Being Used*
- ► *How Should Bonds Be Registered?*
- ► *Purchasing for Special Occasions*
- ► *Bond Series that Can No Longer Be Purchased*
- ► *Bond Investment Growth with Systematic Purchase*

Are people still buying Bonds? You bet. The sale of U.S. Savings Bonds has been robust in recent years. Over $17 billion were sold in 1992 and over $13 billion in 1993. In March 1994, exactly one year after the guaranteed interest rate was lowered to 4%, Bond sales were over $900 million, the third highest sales figure for March in 52 years.

This chapter will walk you through the purchase process. The discussion of interest rates and timing issues is limited to new issues of U.S. Savings Bonds (see Chapters 3 and 4 for details on older Bonds).

An Explanation of Bonds
Available Today

There are two types of Bonds that can be obtained: Series EE and Series HH. The two have very different purposes.

- The Series EE Bond is an interest accrual Bond. The interest it earns becomes part of the value of the Bond. At redemption, you receive the purchase price plus all the interest earned.

- The Series HH Bond is a current income Bond. As the name suggests, this Bond pays an interest payment to the Bond owner every six months. The HH Bond will always be worth the face value at redemption.

The greatest distinction between the two, however, is that *only Series EE Bonds can be bought for cash.* HH Bonds can be obtained only by exchanging Series E or EE Bonds or Savings Notes or by reinvesting eligible H Bonds. For this reason, the bulk of this chapter will deal with the Series EE Bond. Additional information on HH Bonds is provided in Chapter 10.

Before determining where to purchase your Series EE Bonds, you need to determine whether this type of investment is for you. You will want to familiarize yourself with this type of Bond and consider the pros and cons of such a purchase.

The following are Series EE Bond facts:

- It is purchased at half the face value: A $100 Bond costs $50.

- It is guaranteed to reach face value in seventeen years or less. The original maturity period is fixed at seventeen years.

- A new market-based variable rate will be assigned to the Bond at each six-month increase period. The first rate assigned to your Bond if you purchase between May 1, 1995, and October 31, 1995, is 5.25%. For current rate information for new purchases of Series EE Bonds, call 1-800-4USBOND.

- The Bond will earn interest for a total of thirty years from the date of purchase.

- The EE Bond is an interest accrual security. This means interest is added to the value of the Bond periodically. At redemption you receive your purchase price plus the interest.

- The interest you earn is tax-deferred. You may elect to report interest annually; however, most Bond owners do not report interest until they redeem the Bonds. (See Chapter 8 for more tax in-information.)

- Interest earned is subject to federal tax, but exempt from state and local taxes.

- When specific guidelines are met, the Bonds may be tax-free for qualified educational expenses. (See Chapter 9.)

- You may purchase the following denominations: $50, $75, $100, $200, $500, $1,000, $5,000, and $10,000. If you purchase Bonds through payroll deduction, the minimum denomination that you may buy is $100 (Table 12.1).

- The purchase limit is $15,000 per person, per calendar year. (See "Purchase Limitations," later in this chapter.)

Table 12.1

Series EE Bonds by Face Value and Portrait
(issued from 1980 to present)

Issue Price	Face Amount	Portraits
$25.00	$50.00	George Washington
$37.50	$75.00	John Adams
$50.00	$100.00	Thomas Jefferson
$100.00	$200.00	James Madison
$250.00	$500.00	Alexander Hamilton
$500.00	$1,000.00	Benjamin Franklin
$2,500.00	$5,000.00	Paul Revere
$5,000.00	$10,000.00	James Wilson

Adapted from "The Book on U.S. Savings Bonds," p.2.

The Pros and Cons of Purchasing Series EE Bonds

Are Series EE Bonds competitive? Are they a good investment? Ask ten people and you will get ten different answers. An examination of some basic pros and cons can help you think through your position.

Pros

1. No-load to purchase or redeem (no fees to buy or sell your Bonds).

2. You can start with as little as $25.

3. The first new short-term market rate was 5.25%. Current rates may be better than your savings accounts and/or Certificates of Deposit and/or money market funds. Call 1-800-4USBOND for interest rate information for new purchases.

4. They are fully guaranteed by the United States Government.

5. There is no penalty for redemption before maturity.

6. The interest is exempt from state and local taxes.

7. You convert to a long-term market-based variable interest rate if you hold the Bond at least five years. The long-term market rate will generally be higher than the short-term market rate.

8. The principal is secure and interest income is modest.

Cons

1. You must hold the Bonds for six months (no liquidity for six months; some exceptions in extreme emergencies do apply).

2. Purchase limitations of $15,000 per person, per year apply, though this can be exceeded by adding co-owners. Read the section on purchase limitations for an explanation.

3. The short-term market interest rate may be much lower than your expectations or needs.

4. It may take ten to eighteen years to reach face value at current market rates. If the average of your variable rates is 6% during the original maturity period, then the Bonds would reach face value in approximately twelve years. This may not meet your investment goals for doubling your money.

5. Interest is subject to federal tax.

Whether Savings Bonds are right for you will depend on your specific financial situation and your financial goals.

When is the Best Time to Purchase Bonds?

The best time to buy Bonds is late in the month. Why? Whenever you buy a Bond, you begin to earn interest as of the first day of the month in which it was purchased. Therefore, if you purchase on the twenty-fifth or thirtieth of the month, you began to earn interest as of the first business day of that month. This means that you can use your money elsewhere until late in the month, then invest in the EE Bond and be credited with interest as of the first day of the month.

Caution: If you buy late in the month, your funds must be readily available to the bank. Cash, a cashiers check, or a check drawn on the bank you are purchasing through are readily available funds. A check from your money market account, out-of-state, is *not* (it may require a hold period). If you buy on the last day of the month with an out-of-state check, you will likely receive an issue date as of the following month, because that is when the funds will be available to the bank for purchase.

Where and How Can Bonds Be Purchased?

U.S. Savings Bonds can be applied for in-person or through the mail by several different means:

- Most commercial banks
- Some savings & loans
- Some credit unions
- All Federal Reserve Banks (FRB)
- Many companies via the Payroll Savings Plan

Banks, Savings & Loans, and Credit Unions

While the Series EE Savings Bond can be applied for in person at thousands of institutions around the country, it is best to call before you go. Some banks in certain areas of the country no longer sell or service U.S. Savings Bonds.

The institutions that do sell Bonds will provide a Purchase Application for Series EE Bonds (Figure 12.1). You will need to supply the following information on the application:

✓ Name or names to appear on Bond
✓ Social Security number of the first person named on Bond
✓ Mailing address
✓ Number of Bonds to be purchased

Upon receiving your application, the bank or institution will forward it to a regional FRB for processing. The Bond should be mailed to the address you supplied within one to two weeks.

Important to note: In the past, you may have received your Bond the day that you purchased it. During the last few years the government converted to a Regional Delivery System. This means your bank no longer has the actual Bond in stock. They simply take your application and forward it to the FRB for processing. If you are buying for a birthday or holiday, keep in mind that it takes up to three weeks for delivery. In lieu of the Bond, most banks have a certificate that they can give you indicating that a Bond has been purchased and is "on the way" as seen in Figure 12.2.

Figure 12.2   Gift Certificate

Federal Reserve Bank

You may also call or write your FRB for a Bond purchase application. Mail your completed application, with a check, to the FRB in your region. (You will find a listing in Chapter 17.) If you send a personal check, the Bond will be mailed after the check clears.

Payroll Savings Plan

Millions of Americans buy U.S. Savings Bonds through payroll deduction. If this method of purchase interests you, check with the Human Resources, Personnel, or Payroll department of your company to see if they are participating. If your company has a program in place, they will have the necessary forms.

If your company does not offer a payroll deduction program but would like to, there are several options: The company may arrange to have the Bonds printed through a Federal Reserve Bank regional processing site or another qualified issuing agent, or the company may avail itself of Savings Bond-related financial services offered by a third party, such as National Bond & Trust Co., a private company. The author suggests you contact each organization to see which will best serve your needs. See Chapter 17 for additional information about each organization.

Who Can Buy U.S. Savings Bonds?

The information in the following section has been taken, and in some cases adapted for your convenience, from "The Book on U.S. Savings Bonds." Persons eligible to buy and have Bonds inscribed in their names include:

- Residents of the United States, its territories and possessions, and the Commonwealth of Puerto Rico.

- Citizens of the United States residing abroad.

- Civilian employees of the United States, or members of its Armed Services, regardless of residence or citizenship provided they have a Social Security number.

- Residents of Canada or Mexico who work in the United States, but only if the Bonds are purchased on a payroll deduction plan and the owner provides a Social Security account number.

A person who is not listed above may, nevertheless, be designated as co-owner or beneficiary of a Bond—whether original issue or re-issue—unless that person is a resident of an area where the Treasury restricts or regulates the delivery of checks drawn on U.S. funds. Contact your FRB for current information. Such persons who become entitled to Bonds by right of inheritance or otherwise will not have the right to reissue, under Treasury regulations, but may hold the Bonds without change of registration with the right to redeem them when their area of residence changes or current restrictions are lifted. For full details see Treasury Circular, PD Series 3-80, Section 353.6

Series EE Bonds may be bought by individuals, corporations, associations, public or private organizations, fiduciaries, and other investors in their own right. Bonds purchased by a public or private organization cannot have a co-owner or beneficiary listed on the Bond. Likewise an individual Bond owner cannot list an organization of any type on a Savings Bond as their co-owner or beneficiary.

Author's note: This means that you cannot list a charity, church, pet cemetery, or any other organization on a Bond as co-owner or beneficiary.

An Interesting Exception: Gifts to the United States

Some persons buy Bonds with the intent that upon their death the Bonds will become a gift to the United States. This may be done by designating the United States Treasury as either the co-owner or beneficiary. Purchasers should be advised that these Bonds may not be reissued to change such designation, the only exceptions are Series EE or HH Bonds on which the Treasury has been designated as beneficiary.

Author's note: Let's review the math on this one. Based on the fact that the outstanding debt of our nation is $3.3 trillion (1993 figures), and the total dollars of outstanding Bonds is approximately $175 billion, if all Bond owners gift their Bonds to Uncle Sam, and we all die tomorrow (in which case we won't care about the debt), we will have covered 5.2% of the debt. On second thought, let's review that balanced budget legislation.

Purchase Limitations

The maximum purchase allowed for Series EE Bonds is $15,000 per person, per calendar year ($30,000 face value). This means that you can buy $15,000 on December 30th and another $15,000 on January 2nd. This would use the limitations for each year in which Series EE were bought. However, if you purchase in the name of yourself "or" either your wife or husband, you may now buy double that amount—$30,000 per year. (You are combining your limitation of $15,000 and your spouse's limitation of $15,000.) Do you want to invest another $15,000?

Buy with your son or daughter as a co-owner and use his or her $15,000 limitation.

Caution: Remember that anyone you name as a co-owner on your Bond can cash that Bond without your consent. Give careful consideration to whom you name as co-owner on any Bonds you purchase.

Why are there limitations on the amount you can purchase? Originally, the intent was to keep the Bond program directed toward the individual investor. Limitations keep large blocks of money from one entity from entering and exiting the Bond program. For instance, a company cannot buy $10 million of U.S. Savings Bonds. It is strange that the limits have not been raised since 1980. It would seem logical that they be adjusted upward every five to ten years, especially since the government, from all indications, could use the extra money (or *has* used the extra money). The author's office receives numerous calls each year from Bond owners expressing a desire to purchase more Bonds if the limit would allow. If you would like to see the limit raised, voice your opinion to:

The Department of the Treasury
Bureau of the Public Debt
Savings Bond Marketing Office
Washington, D.C. 20226

How to Compute whose Purchase Limit is Being Used

The next section is fairly technical and is also taken from "The Book on U.S. Savings Bonds." For full details on these matters, see Treasury Circular PD Series 3-80, Section 353.10-11.

Co-ownership Issues

As discussed, the annual limit on Bond purchases is $30,000 face amount and $15,000 issue price for Series EE Bonds. In computing this limit, Bonds registered in the names of two persons as co-owners may be applied to the holdings of either co-owner or apportioned between them, up to a maximum of $60,000, face amount, in EE Bonds.

Each co-owner may, in addition, purchase and hold in that calendar year Bonds bearing either of their names with other persons as co-owners up to a maximum of $30,000 face amount, per co-owner, as long as these additional co-owners do not have other Bonds purchased in that year bearing their names as owner or co-owner.

Beneficiary Issues

Purchases are applied to the owner, not beneficiary.

Fiduciary Capacity

Bonds held by a person serving as guardian or another fiduciary capacity are computed separately from personal purchases.

No Cumulative Limits

The purchase limit applies to Bonds issued in any one calendar year; purchases may be added to Bonds obtained in previous years. Bonds purchased and redeemed in the same calendar year may also be excluded from computation.

How Should Bonds Be Registered?

U.S. Savings Bonds are registered securities. This means that the name of the person or entity entitled to the Bonds is printed on the face of the Bond.

The three most common forms of registration are single ownership, co-ownership, and owner with beneficiary.

Single Ownership

As the name implies, only one person is listed on the Bond as owner.

S.S. # 123-45-6789
John S. Anybody
123 Bond Ave.
Interest, NY 11001

Co-ownership

Two persons are listed on the Bond as co-owners. Either party can cash the Bond *without* the other party's consent. Co-ownership means equal ownership. If you choose to put another person on your Bond, make sure you are comfortable with having them as a co-owner. Upon the death of one co-owner, the remaining co-owner becomes the sole owner of the Bond. The Bonds can be reissued to remove the deceased party's name and to add a new co-owner or beneficiary.

> S.S. # 123-45-6789
> John S. Anybody
> 123 Bond Ave.
> Interest, NY 11001
>
> OR Mary B. Anybody

Beneficiary

This form of ownership allows for one owner and one beneficiary to be listed on the Bonds. The owner may cash the Bond at any time (after the first six months). The beneficiary may cash the Bonds only after providing a death certificate of the owner. The beneficiary is listed as the "POD" (Pay on Death). This does *not* mean that the Bond *must* be cashed upon the death of the owner; however, the Bond cannot be negotiated by the person named as POD until the owner is deceased. The registration appears as follows:

> S.S. # 123-45-6789
> John S. Anybody
> 123 Bond Ave.
> Interest, NY 11001
>
> POD Mary B. Anybody

The maximum number of names on a Bond is two, regardless of the form of registration. You cannot have two co-owners *and* a beneficiary.

Purchasing for Special Occasions

Bonds now take up to three weeks to be delivered to you. Thus you must plan ahead when buying for special occasions (birthdays, holidays, graduations). If you do get stuck purchasing a Bond a few days before the important occasion, ask the bank to provide a certificate of purchase that you can give, indicating that a Bond is on the way.

The purchase application will ask for the Social Security number of the first-named party on the Bond. If you do not know that number, you may provide your number. However, this means that your number will appear on the Bond. This does not create any tax liability for you, since the person who redeems the Bond is required to supply their

Social Security number at the time of redemption. The person redeeming the Bond is supposed to get the 1099-INT. However, the fact that your Social Security number is on the Bond may lead some bank tellers to incorrectly assign the 1099-INT to that number. Your best bet is to call the recipient's family and obtain the correct Social Security number.

The purchase application also asks for the "mail to" address on the Bond. If you are buying a gift and you list your name and address under "mail to," then your name and address will appear on the Bond. (Bonds are mailed in window envelopes.) Thus, there will be three names on the Bond. However, only the first-named party and the designated co-owner or beneficiary are entitled to the Bond. The "mail to" person is not entitled to the Bond. This will inevitably cause some confusion down the road but it is unavoidable under the present system.

Note: You may not want to list the bank as the "mail to" address. If you do, the bank name and address will appear on the Bond.

Gift Giving

This is a matter of long-term versus short-term gratification. How many times have you purchased a new toy, only to be disappointed at the reaction of the cute little urchin who ignored it while playing with the box it came in? Savings Bonds are a gift that most children will appreciate in the future. And unlike most toys, a Bond will grow in value over time.

Bonds purchased in the past used to have the word "gift" typed on the Bond. This had no special significance in relationship to the value, interest rates or ownership of the Bond, it merely indicated that the Bond was given to the owner as a gift. With the new system of delivery, Bonds are no longer being inscribed with the word "gift." (See Chapter 14, "Recent Changes in the Bond Program and How They Affect You.")

Bond Series that Can No Longer Be Purchased

In addition to bridges and swampland in Florida, avoid anyone who tries to sell you the following series of Bonds: They are no longer being sold.

Table 12.2

Bond Series No Longer For Sale

Series	Issue Period	Comment on Final Maturity
Series A-D	March 1935 - April 1941	All Series A-D Bonds have stopped earning interest.
Series E	May 1941 - June 1980	Some, not all, Series E Bonds have stopped earning interest. See Chapter 6 for details.
Series F & G	May 1941 - April 1952	All Series F & G Bonds have stopped earning interest.
Series H	June 1952 - Dec. 1979	Series H Bonds over 30 years old have stopped paying interest.
Series J & K	May 1952 - April 1957	All Series J & K Bonds have stopped earning interest.
Savings Notes	May 1967 - October 1970	The Savings Notes will stop earning interest 30 years from the date of purchase.

Adapted from "The Book on U.S. Savings Bonds," p.8.

If you own Series A to D, F, G, J, or K Bonds, contact your regional FRB or the BPD for disposition instructions. Chapter 17 lists the appropriate addresses and telephone numbers.

Bond Investment Growth with Systematic Purchase

Millions of Americans have successfully used Bonds to build or supplement their savings. Table 12.3 illustrates what you can expect under several different scenarios. The table outlines projected savings at interest rates of 4%, 5%, 6%, and 7%. The 4% interest rate is the guaranteed minimum for eighteen years on Series EE Bonds issued from March 1993 to April 1995. The 6% interest rate is the guaranteed minimum for twelve years on Series EE Bonds issued from November 1986 to February 1993. (These Bonds must be held at least five years to receive this guarantee.) Current issues of Series EE Bonds do not have a guaranteed rate. However, if the current rules had been in effect over the last five years, these Bonds would have returned about 4.1%.

Figure 12.1

Purchase Application for
Series EE Bonds

PD F 5263
Dept. of the Treasury
Bur. of the Public Debt
(Revised February 1991)

ORDER FOR SERIES EE U.S. SAVINGS BONDS

OMB No. 1535-0084
Expires 9-30-91

PLEASE FOLLOW THE INSTRUCTIONS ON THE BACK WHEN COMPLETING THIS PURCHASE ORDER.

1. **OWNER OR FIRST-NAMED COOWNER (Bonds registered to)**

   Name

   Soc. Sec. No. — —

2. **BONDS TO BE DELIVERED "CARE OF"** (Do not complete this section unless name is different from the owner or first-named coowner in section 1 above.)

   Mail to:

3. **ADDRESS WHERE BONDS ARE TO BE DELIVERED**

   (NUMBER AND STREET OR RURAL ROUTE)

   (CITY OR TOWN)   (STATE)   (ZIP CODE)

4. **COOWNER OR BENEFICIARY** Coownership will be assumed if neither or if both blocks are checked (See #4 on back).
   The following person is to be named as   coowner   beneficiary

   Name

5. **BONDS ORDERED**

Denom.	Quantity	Issue Price	Total Issue Price	FOR AGENT USE ONLY
$ 50		X $ 25.00	= $	
$ 75		X $ 37.50	= $	
$ 100		X $ 50.00	= $	
$ 200		X $ 100.00	= $	
$ 500		X $ 250.00	= $	
$ 1,000		X $ 500.00	= $	
$ 5,000		X $ 2,500.00	= $	
$ 10,000		X $ 5,000.00	= $	
TOTAL ISSUE PRICE OF PURCHASE			$	AFFIXED AGENT STAMP CERTIFIES THAT TOTAL AMOUNT OF PURCHASE IS CORRECT

6. **DATE PURCHASE ORDER AND PAYMENT PRESENTED TO AGENT**

   (MO.)   (DAY)   (YR.)

7. **SIGNATURE**

   PURCHASER'S SIGNATURE

   ( )

   PURCHASER'S NAME, IF OTHER THAN OWNER OR FIRST-NAMED COOWNER. (Please print)   DAYTIME TELEPHONE NUMBER

   STREET ADDRESS (If not shown above)   CITY   STATE   ZIP CODE

SEE INSTRUCTIONS FOR PRIVACY ACT AND PAPERWORK REDUCTION ACT NOTICE

FRB COPY

Systematic Purchase Pattern

Table 12.3

| | Estimated Value of Savings Bond Investment at the End of... | | | | | | | |
| | Five Years | | Ten Years | | Twenty Years | | Thirty Years | |
	4%	5%	4%	5%	4%	5%	4%	5%
Save $25 month, purchase $150 of EE Bonds every six months.	$1,642	$1,680	$3,644	$3,831	$9,060	$10,110	$17,107	$20,398
Save $50 month, purchase $300 of EE Bonds every six months.	$3,284	$3,361	$7,289	$7,663	$18,120	$20,220	$34,215	$40,797
Save $100 month, purchase $600 of EE Bonds every six months.	$6,569	$6,722	$14,578	$15,326	$36,241	$40,441	$68,430	$81,595
Save $200 month, purchase $1,200 of EE Bonds every six months.	$13,139	$13,444	$29,156	$30,653	$72,482	$80,883	$136,861	$163,189
Save $500 month, purchase $3,000 of EE Bonds every six months.	$32,849	$33,610	$72,892	$76,633	$181,205	$202,207	$342,154	$407,974

The calculations in the above table are based on the following assumptions:

1. The Bond purchaser will save money at an even monthly rate and will purchase Bonds twice a year. A monthly purchase pattern will result in a slightly higher final value.
2. That the interest rates used to calculate future values will be consistent over the time period the calculations were made.
3. The money invested is the purchase price of the Bonds, not the face value. Thus the term "purchase $300 of Bonds every six months" means $300 purchase price, $600 face value. (Remember EE Bonds are purchased for one-half the face value.)
4. The guaranteed interest rate for Series EE Bonds purchased March 1, 1993 to April 30, 1995, is 4 percent for the original maturity period. There is no guaranteed rate for Series EE Bonds purchased after April 30, 1995. Call 1-800-USBONDS for rate information on current purchases.

Note: This table does not guarantee a specific return on any investment you make. Market conditions and rules governing the Savings Bond program may change without notice. Obtain current rate information and complete details before making any investment.

Systematic Purchase Pattern

Table 12.3 cont.

	Estimated Value of Savings Bond Investment at the End of…							
	Five Years		Ten Years		Twenty Years		Thirty Years	
	6%	7%	6%	7%	6%	7%	6%	7%
Save $25 month, purchase $150 of EE Bonds every six months.	$1,720	$1,760	$4,031	$4,242	$11,310	$12,682	$24,458	$29,478
Save $50 month, purchase $300 of EE Bonds every six months.	$3,439	$3,519	$8,061	$8,484	$22,620	$25,365	$48,916	$58,955
Save $100 month, purchase $600 of EE Bonds every six months.	$6,878	$7,038	$16,122	$16,968	$45,241	$50,730	$97,832	$117,910
Save $200 month, purchase $1,200 of EE Bonds every six months.	$13,756	$14,076	$32,244	$33,936	$90,482	$101,460	$195,664	$235,820
Save $500 month, purchase $3,000 of EE Bonds every six months.	$34,392	$35,194	$80,611	$84,839	$226,203	$253,650	$489,160	$589,550

The calculations in the above table are based the following assumptions:

1. The Bond purchaser will save money at an even monthly rate and will purchase Bonds twice a year. A monthly purchase pattern will result in a slightly higher final value.
2. That the interest rates used to calculate future values will be consistent over the time period the calculations were made.
3. The money invested is the purchase price of the Bonds, not the face value. Thus the term "purchase $300 of Bonds every six months" means $300 purchase price, $600 face value. (Remember EE Bonds are purchased for one-half the face value.)
4. The guaranteed interest rate for Series EE Bonds purchased March 1, 1993 to April 30, 1995, is 4 percent for the original maturity period. There is no guaranteed rate for Series EE Bonds purchased after April 30, 1995. Call 1-800-USBONDS for rate information on current purchases.

Note: This table does not guarantee a specific return on any investment you make. Market conditions and rules governing the Savings Bond program may change without notice. Obtain current rate information and complete details before making any investment.

_____ Chapter 13

REDEEMING U.S. SAVINGS BONDS

> ▸ *Where Can Bonds Be Cashed?*
> ▸ *Who Is Eligible to Cash a Particular Bond?*
> ▸ *What Are the Tax Consequences?*
> ▸ *What Should Be Considered Prior to Redemption?*

"What's the big deal?" many Bond owners ask. "I'll just cash my Bonds whenever I need the money." After reading these two true stories, you will understand what the "big deal" is.

A Sad Story

John was a blue collar worker who purchased Bonds regularly through the Payroll Savings Plan. His family knew he was buying Bonds, but they never realized how many he had until after his death. They were surprised to find 180 Savings Bonds. Those advising John's wife suggested that she cash the Bonds. She did just that. Late in November she redeemed 180 Bonds, worth a total of almost $60,000. What she was not told, and what she did not realize, was that 30 of the Bonds were due to increase December 1st. Thus, by holding the Bonds only a few more days, she could have pocketed an additional $300 to $375. Not only that, holding another specific group of 30 Bonds until January 1st would have netted her another $300 to $375. As with most

Bond owners, she did not realize how important it is to time the redemption of Savings Bonds.

A Happier Story

Betty works for a local school district. She saved her money, much of it in Savings Bonds, and she planned to purchase a condominium. She had only eight Bonds, but each had a face value of $10,000! In June, Betty found a condominium she liked; she signed a purchase agreement and the closing was set for September. She was not sure whether to cash her Bonds immediately or wait until nearer the closing date. To address her question, she chose to have her Bonds analyzed. She discovered that six of the Bonds, with a redemption value of $50,000, were due to increase September 1st. By waiting until September to cash the Bonds, she would receive $1,500 more than if she cashed them in June. She also discovered that the remaining two Bonds had increased in value June 1st, and would not increase again until December. She cashed those last two Bonds immediately and put the money into an interest-bearing account.

Betty was thrilled to have the extra $1,500. Before learning about her Bonds, she had planned on just cashing them all during June or July.

As you can see, careful planning can be very advantageous when you think about redeeming U.S. Savings Bonds. This chapter is devoted to covering all the issues you need to consider.

Where Can Bonds Be Cashed?

All Federal Reserve Banks (FRB) can redeem Savings Bonds, although the Bureau of the Public Debt (BPD) may handle some cases that require legal rulings. Bonds may be redeemed at thousands of commercial banks across America and at some savings & loans and credit unions, as well.

The easiest place to start is with your local bank, but *call* first. Ask your bank if they redeem U.S. Savings Bonds. If they do not, try another bank.

Remember, the bank's role is to give you the money that you are due when you present the Bond for redemption. They are not required to advise you on timing issues, nor are they particularly good at it. (For a full explanation, see Chapter 2, "Banks and Bonds.") It is ultimately the responsibility of the Bond owner to choose the moment to submit a Bond for redemption.

Who Is Eligible to Cash a Particular Bond?

A person cashing a Bond needs to have valid identification. At least one valid piece of the following identification is necessary for redemptions of under $1,000 where you are not known by the bank:

General
✓ Current operator's license
✓ State identification card
✓ Employer identification card

Governmental
✓ Armed Forces identification card
✓ United States passport
✓ Federal employee identification card

The type of identification and specific requirements depend on the dollar amount of the transaction and how familiar you are to the bank. Call before you go to see if your bank has additional or fewer requirements. Typically, the bank is the big loser if Bonds are cashed by a person who is not entitled. For that reason, bank personnel are required to ensure that the person redeeming a Bond is entitled to the funds.

In Chapter 12, various options for registering a Bond were presented. The registration choice made when the Bond was purchased determines who is eligible to redeem the Bond.

If the Bond is in one name only, and that person is living, he or she is the only one who can cash the Bond. (Some exceptions may apply in power of attorney cases. However, a local bank will not redeem in power of attorney cases; those must be forwarded to the Bureau of the Public Debt for a ruling.)

If the Bond is in co-ownership form, either co-owner may cash it without the other's consent. The person cashing the Bond will supply his or her Social Security number and will receive a 1099-INT for interest earned.

If the Bond is registered in one name with another person listed as the beneficiary, then only the first-named party may cash the Bond. Upon the death of the first-named party, the beneficiary may cash the Bond. A death certificate for the first-named party is required for a beneficiary to cash a Bond.

For rulings regarding personal representatives of an estate, call your regional FRB.

The person submitting Bonds for redemption is required to sign the back of each Bond. When there are numerous Bonds and it would be difficult for the Bond owner to negotiate numerous signatures, PD F 1522 (Figure 13.1) may be used to list all the Bonds; the Bond owner need sign only once. Read the instructions thoroughly before attempting to use this form.

What Are the Tax Consequences?

For Series E and EE Bonds and Savings Notes (SNs), redemption is when you receive the interest that has accrued. The interest income earned is deferred until the Bond is cashed or until the Bond reaches final maturity, whichever comes first. In most cases, owners of Series E and EE Bonds and SNs have not reported interest earnings prior to redemption. Thus, when the Bond is redeemed, the owner creates a taxable event. The one exception is when a person has chosen to report interest earned on an annual basis. (See Chapter 8, "Taxation Issues for U.S. Savings Bonds," for more information on that option.)

The bank that redeems the Bond has two basic responsibilities related to the 1099-INT. First, they must provide a copy of the 1099-INT to the person who redeemed the Bond. Some banks do this on the spot; others mail all 1099-INT forms at the end of the year (only interest payments totaling more than $10 need to be reported). Second, they must report the interest earned, name, and Social Security number for each transaction to the IRS. This is normally done in one file at the end of the year.

When a Series E or EE Bond or SN is redeemed, the bank will require that the person redeeming the Bond supply his or her Social Security number. The bank will not (or should not) automatically use the number printed on the Bond.

Conflicting Government Rules

Regarding interest responsibility, the rules outlined in IRS and Treasury Department literature and what really happens when banks report interest income are not exactly "in sync." The Treasury Department publication "Legal Aspects of U.S. Savings Bonds" (1993, p.4) states that "the principal owner" (defined as "the person whose funds were used to purchase the Bonds") bears the tax liability. However, the data collection and reporting systems are not set up to support this statement. In reality, the person who redeems the Bonds receives the 1099-INT. Thus, if John Q. Public bought a Bond with his son as the co-owner and his son redeems the Bond, the bank will ask for the son's Social Security number and will issue the 1099-INT to the son. IRS has no idea whose funds were used to purchase the Bonds; they expect the son to report the interest that the bank reported under his Social Security number. The IRS rules state that the person receiving the 1099-INT should then issue a 1099 to the principal owner and to IRS. However, in the years that the author has worked with Bond owners, he has never met one Bond owner who was aware of this IRS rule. (This topic is covered in more detail in Chapter 8.)

Important: Make a note of the interest earned on your Bond at the time of redemption. Put this note (or the 1099-INT, if the bank supplied one) with your tax papers for that calendar year. Many Bond owners cash Bonds early in the year and forget that they have interest income to report. The Bond owner may lose, misfile, or never remember receiving a 1099-INT and fail to report the interest on their annual tax return. But guess who makes a habit of making sure you remember—that's right, your friends at the IRS. The bank supplies them with a copy of the same 1099-INT information that you receive. The IRS does a simple computer check to see if the amount you reported matches the amount they think you should have reported. If the numbers don't match, you are a likely candidate for some communication from the IRS.

Interest earned on Bonds is subject to federal tax but is exempt from state and local tax. In some cases, if the Bond qualifies for the education feature, the interest might be tax-free. (Refer to the educational feature guidelines in Chapter 9.)

What Should Be Considered Prior to Redemption?

Selective Redemption

Now is the time to study your alternatives. Do not wait until your back is against the wall and you must liquidate your Bonds immediately. Those situations do happen, so advance planning can be a great benefit.

In the next few pages, we will examine a practice called "Selective Redemption." It is built upon a simple premise: *At a given point in time it may make more sense to cash one particular Bond rather than another.*

The concept of selective redemption was first presented in Chapter 10 as an alternative to exchanging for HH Bonds. In this chapter, selective redemption is applied to a typical redemption situation.

Selective redemption is an alternative to randomly redeeming large groups of U.S. Savings Bonds. If you randomly redeem your Bonds, it is unlikely that you will maximize your Savings Bond potential.

From Chapter 6, "Tracking Your Investment," you learned that each Bond you own carries a unique set of information. Tracking your Bonds, whether you do it yourself or secure the services of The Savings Bond Informer, enables you to analyze the data for each Bond that you own. You will be able to compare the data and determine which Bonds to redeem at any given point in time. If you have a completed Bond Statement, you may want to refer to it during this discussion.

In evaluating your Bonds, you should consider several factors.

1. What rate of interest applies to each Bond?
2. When do each of my Bonds increase in value?
3. What is the accrued interest on each Bond?
4. What is the value of each Bond?
5. How much interest-earning life is left in each Bond?

It is important to note that each Bond owner may place a different priority on the above questions. For one Bond owner, minimizing the amount of interest income that will have to be reported may be highest objective (#3). For another, keeping Bonds that have the longest life left may be most important (#5). For yet another, the priority may be in keeping the Bonds that are paying the highest rate of interest and redeeming the Bonds paying a lower one (#1).

The Best Time of the Month to Cash Bonds

Always cash your Bonds early in the month. If your Bond is due to increase in July and you redeem it July 1, you will be credited with the July increase. If you hold that same Bond until July 30, you will receive the same amount as you would have on July 1.

The Best Time of Year to Cash Bonds

If you are thinking of redeeming Bonds toward the end of a calendar year, you may want to consider waiting until after January 1. That way you will have one additional year before you must report the interest. In some cases it makes sense to redeem some Bonds at the end of one year and other Bonds at the beginning of the next. This will spread the tax liability over two years.

Avoid the Personal Horror Story

Most people have held their Bonds for a long period of time. It does not make sense to collect Bonds for twenty years and then suddenly cash them all on the same day. Allow time for an analysis of the options available to you before redemption. Knowing your options will help you get maximum return on your Savings Bond investment.

Figure 13.1

Request for Payment PD F 1522

PD F 1522
Department of the Treasury
Bureau of the Public Debt
(Revised October 1992)

SPECIAL FORM OF REQUEST FOR PAYMENT OF
UNITED STATES SAVINGS AND RETIREMENT SECURITIES
WHERE USE OF A DETACHED REQUEST IS AUTHORIZED

OMB No. 1535-0004
Expires 10-31-94

IMPORTANT: Follow instructions in filling out this form. You should be aware that the making of any false, fictitious or fraudulent claim to the United States is a crime punishable by imprisonment of not more than five years or a fine up to $250,000, or both, under 18 U.S.C. 287 and 18 U.S.C. 3571. Additionally, 31 U.S.C. 3729 provides for civil penalties for the maker of a false or fraudulent claim to the United States of an amount not less than $5,000 and not more than $10,000, plus treble the amount of the Government's damages as an additional sanction.
PRINT IN INK OR TYPE ALL INFORMATION

I am the owner or person entitled to payment of the following-described securities which bear the name(s)

of _____ and hereby request payment.

_____
(This line for use in case of partial redemption only. See paragraph 4 of Instructions.)

SERIAL NUMBER	ISSUE DATE	SERIAL NUMBER	ISSUE DATE	SERIAL NUMBER	ISSUE DATE

(If space is insufficient, use continuation sheet, sign it, and refer to it above. PD F 3500 may be used for this purpose.)

_____   OR   _____
Social Security Account Number   Employer Identification Number

**Sign in ink in presence
of certifying officer ▶** _____

Daytime Telephone Number _____
Address
(For delivery of check) _____
(Number and street or rural route)   (City or town)   (State)   (ZIP Code)

I CERTIFY that the above-named person, whose identity is well-known or proved to me, personally appeared before me this _____ day of _____, 19 _____, at _____
(City)   (State)

and signed the above request, acknowledging the same to be his/her free act and deed.

*(OFFICIAL STAMP
OR SEAL)*

_____
(Signature and title of certifying officer)

_____
(Address)

(SEE INSTRUCTIONS ON REVERSE)

SEE INSTRUCTIONS FOR PRIVACY ACT AND PAPERWORK REDUCTION ACT NOTICE

RECENT CHANGES
IN THE BOND PROGRAM
AND HOW THEY AFFECT YOU

▸ *A Change in the Guaranteed Interest Rate (1993)*
▸ *The Impact of the 1993 Rate Change*
▸ *A New Method of Distribution (late 1980s to 1995)*
▸ *New Reissuing Sites (1992-1995)*
▸ *GATT Legislation and Its Impact (1994-1995)*

Change is the operative word in today's world and the Savings Bond program is no exception. Many recent changes have impacted Bond owners.

A Change in the Guaranteed
Interest Rate (1993)

On Saturday, February 27, 1993, with unexpected brevity and no prior notice, the U.S. Treasury lowered the guaranteed interest rate on U.S.

Savings Bonds. In the words of one media person, "...the last one out on Saturday sent the fax (press release) and shut off the lights."

Thousands of Bond owners voiced their displeasure at the way this guaranteed rate change was handled. They were given no opportunity to engage, or change, any position related to their Bond holdings. This was particularly upsetting to retirees who had planned to exchange for HH Bonds at 6%, but were now forced to the new rate of 4%.

In 1986, when the guaranteed interest rate was to drop from 7.5% to 6%, Bond owners were given a three- to four-business day advance warning. This enabled literally tens of thousands of Bond owners to submit their purchase and exchange applications before the change took effect, severely overtaxing the system in the process. This set a certain precedent and consumers came to expect the same series of events.

Another factor made the 1993 sudden drop surprising: The two changes in the guaranteed rate prior to March 1, 1993, (November 1986 and November 1982) both occurred in the same month that the variable interest rate is announced. Many people assumed that all changes would occur in either May or November. Surprise, surprise.

Revisiting 1986: The author was supervising the Savings Bond Division at the Federal Reserve Bank (FRB) of Chicago, Detroit Branch, at the time. That office was averaging about fifty Bond purchase applications a day. When the rate change was announced, the Detroit office received over 10,000 applications in three days. Banks complained that all they were doing was selling Bonds and indeed they were. The FRBs of Chicago and New York each reported over 50,000 purchase applications in that three-day period. It took the FRBs several months to process this volume that was about 200 times the normal level.

In 1992, Savings Bond sales were at an all time high of $17.7 billion. Their popularity seemed to be driven not by patriotism but by a guaranteed interest rate of 6%. The 6% was about twice what some Certificates of Deposit or savings accounts were paying. Obviously, the banks were not very happy with this state of affairs.

The pressure was on for the federal government to lower the guaranteed interest rate and for good reason. Why should the government pay more to borrow money than it has to? What about banks that are doing the government a service by selling a product that is more attractive than some of their own products? As interest rates in the marketplace continued to drop, many correctly anticipated a drop in the Savings Bond guaranteed rate.

Rather than endure a repeat performance of purchase application inundation (in the midst of major consolidation operations), the government chose to make the announcement over the weekend, providing no window of opportunity for the consumer.

This strategy certainly worked from an operations standpoint. On Monday, following the announcement, one could assume that volumes were normal at best, maybe even below normal, due to the decreased rate. As for the public relations aspect of such a move, the outcome remains to be seen. The Savings Bond Informer, Inc., received numerous calls complaining about the way this change was handled. Several callers voiced their intent to end their participation in the Bond program. Only time and sales will tell if the public relations damage was short or long term.

For the person who was purchasing Bonds as a short-term investment (one to two years) not much had changed. Why? The new guaranteed rate of 4% was effective immediately upon the purchase of the Bond. Whether a Bond is held six months, a year or two years, there is a guaranteed 4%. Under the old guaranteed rate of 6%, the Bond had to be held five years to get 6%. If the Bond was held less than five years, it started out at 4.16% for the first six months, 4.27% for the first year and 4.64% if held for two years. As you can see, the change for the short-term investor was not as significant as many believed.

The Impact of the 1993 Rate Change

Lowering the interest rate from 6% to 4% had an immediate impact on all EE Bonds purchased, or HH Bonds obtained through exchange, and all Bonds that entered an extended maturity period between March 1, 1993, and April 30, 1995.

EE Bonds

All EE Bonds purchased between March 1, 1993, and April 30, 1995, will now earn a fixed rate of 4% for the first five years. Once the EE Bond is held for five years, it is eligible for the average variable interest rate, which may be higher than 4%. There is no graduated scale during the first five years of EE Bond ownership. The 4% is in effect whether you hold the Bond six months (the minimum required) or four years. If the Bond is held for five years, and the average variable interest rate is less than 4%, that Bond will still earn the minimum of 4%.

At 4%, an EE Bond will take eighteen years to reach face value. This same Bond will continue to draw interest for a full thirty years from the date of purchase. The other significant difference is that the EE Bond, held six months, will increase in value *monthly,* not semi-annually, until the Bond is five years old. After five years if the average variable rate is greater than 4%, the Bond will convert to a semi-annual increase pattern. This monthly increase only applies to Bonds purchased between March 1, 1993 and April 30, 1995; *it does not apply to Bonds issued prior to March 1, 1993 that are at least thirty months old*, nor does it apply to Bonds issued after April 30, 1995.

HH Bonds

HH Bonds obtained through exchanging Series E and EE Bonds or Savings Notes after March 1, 1993, pay a fixed rate of 4% (a new rate for new issues can be announced by the government at any time) for the first ten years. An HH Bond will earn interest up to twenty years from the date of issue. After the first ten years, the Bond will enter a ten-year extension picking up the current guaranteed rate at that time. Since 1989 (when direct deposit became mandatory for new exchanges), holders of HH Bonds receive an interest payment, direct deposited to their bank account, every six months.

Older Savings Bonds

Older Savings Bonds will be affected only as they enter a new extended maturity period. See Chapter 4 for a full explanation.

A New Method of Distribution
(late 1980s to 1995)

As introduced in Chapter 12, "Purchasing U.S. Savings Bonds," the last five years have brought significant changes in the distribution of U.S. Savings Bonds, which, in turn, has affected the time that customers must wait to receive their Bonds.

In the 1980s, Savings Bonds could be obtained either the day of purchase or within one day of submission of the purchase application. This was great for the customer who wanted to buy a Bond today for a birthday tomorrow.

Having blank stock at thousands of locations, however, required time-consuming monthly balancing between the local banks and the FRBs.

In the late 1980s, the Treasury began to implement the Regional Delivery System (RDS). This meant that banks would no longer carry blank stock or type the Savings Bond. Instead, the bank would focus on the point of sale, taking both application and funds from the customer. The applications and funds are then transferred to the

Federal Reserve Bank. The Federal Reserve Bank holds and imprints the Bond stock and ensures that the Bonds are mailed.

The Bond owner has been affected in three ways. First, now it takes up to three weeks after purchase to receive a Bond. Second, the word "gift" is no longer printed on the Bond. This term had no significance, other than being something the Bond purchaser liked to see. The third effect is that the address to which the Bonds are delivered now appears on the Bond along with the owner's name. Therefore, you may see a Bond inscribed as follows:

John Doe

mail to: Sally Smith
        123 Anywhere
        Somewhere, GA   12345

OR Sam Doe

The third name, which appears between the names of the two rightful owners, may produce some confusion to Bond owners or bank tellers upon redemption. To the unknowing eye, it would appear that Sally Smith has some entitlement to the Bond. As stated in Chapter 12, she does not.

New Reissuing Sites (1992-1995)

Within the last decade the BPD has been implementing consolidation of Bond activities at fewer FRBs. The idea is to reduce again the number of locations that carry Bond stock and, subsequently, the number of locations that must be monitored. They have realized they can save substantial time and money through consolidation.

This is why we now have five sites nationwide that reissue Savings Bonds. The FRB in Los Angeles and San Francisco forward all of their Bond activity to Kansas City. Many major cities—New York, Boston, Chicago, and Los Angeles—were not selected for increased volume and operation.

The change to you as a Bond owner is somewhat transparent. If you want to have Bonds reissued, you send them to the FRB that services your state. The only way you will know where your Bonds are actually printed is by the little stamp below the issue date. If it reads FRB K.C., the Bond was printed in Kansas City. For information on the FRB that serves your area, see Chapter 17.

GATT Legislation and Its Impact (1994-1995)

The years 1994 and 1995 brought the most significant changes to the U.S. Savings Bond program in over fifty years.

In December 1994, the General Agreement on Trade and Tariffs (also known as GATT) was passed. This legislation granted the Treasury Department authority to change the current guaranteed rate structure. Effective May 1, 1995, new rules were implemented.

What Happened?

What does the GATT have to do with U.S. Savings Bonds? At first glance a person would certainly be hard pressed to find a connection. However, GATT required several funding options and believe it or not, Savings Bonds were thrown into the hopper as one of the ways the government will pay for GATT.

Some may have thought this was a last-minute effort to include Savings Bonds. Not so. The Treasury Department had wanted to make changes in the Bond program for several years. This legislation was a convenient way to gain the legislative authority necessary to rework the Bond program.

Why did the government want to rework the Bond program? Under the old rules (prior to May 1, 1995), the Bond program promised a guaranteed rate for each Bond in the original or extended maturity periods (see Chapter 4 for more details on maturity periods). This guaranteed rate often left the Treasury in a position that was out of sync with market conditions. For example, in 1993 the Treasury was paying 7.5% on Bonds bought in 1985, while market conditions for conservative investments were as low as 2-3%. Clearly they were paying more than they would have liked. Conversely, in 1994, Savings Bonds offered a guaranteed rate of 4%, while other conservative investments were paying over 6%. This hurt the sale of new Bonds, and left the Bond program in an unattractive competitive position. This increased the desire to go to a system that would allow the Bond interest rates to follow market conditions up and down, creating a more competitive product.

When Did This Happen?

Timeline of the changes:

August 1994—Initial indications that GATT includes important legislation that will impact the Savings Bond program
December 1994—GATT passes

March 1995—Treasury announces new changes in Bond program as a result of new authority granted in GATT, scheduled for May 1 implementation.

May 1995—Actual implementation of changes announced in March. First time a short-term variable rate is announced (5.25%). Elimination of retroactive and averaging features of long-term variable rate for new purchases of Series EE Bonds.

Whom Does This Impact?

The "New Rules" apply to any person who buys a Series EE Bond after April 30, 1995. Bonds purchased prior to May 1, 1995, are not affected by the new rules. HH Bonds are not affected by the new rules. Only new purchases of Series EE Bonds will be affected.

What is the Bottom Line?

These changes should make the Bond program easier to follow and understand. For Bond owners who purchase both before and after the new rules go into effect, the changes may be a bit perplexing because you now need to understand two sets of rules. However, the new rules are a lot easier to understand than the old rules.

What Changed?

1. The guaranteed rate was eliminated for Series EE Bonds issued May 1, 1995, and after.
2. A new short-term variable rate was assigned to Series EE Bonds purchased May 1, 1995, and after. The short-term rate will be 85% of the average of the six-month Treasury Bill yields for a three-month period immediately preceding May 1 and November 1.
3. The retroactive and averaging features of the long-term variable rate have been eliminated (see Chapter 3).
4. There is now a return to semi-annual increase periods for new Series EE Bonds issued after April 30, 1995. (EE Bonds purchased from March 1, 1993, to April 30, 1995, increased in value monthly for the first five years.)
5. The government still has a guarantee although they avoid the use of the word "guarantee." Basically they promise an automatic make-up at year seventeen, if a Bond has not yet reached face value. This computes to a guarantee of about 4.12% over the seventeen-year period. Note, however, that this make-up will only go into effect if two conditions are met. First, the Bond must be held seventeen years. Second, the value of the Bond needs to be less than

face value at year seventeen. If the value of the Bond is above face value, no additional make-up will be added to the Bond.

6. The original maturity period for Series EE Bonds purchased after April 30, 1995 is now seventeen years instead of the eighteen years for Series EE Bonds purchased between March 1, 1993, and April 30, 1995.

An evaluation of the new rules, and a comparison of the new rules vs. the old rules, is offered in Chapter 15.

Change can be a scary word. To this day, the author still does not know how to program his VCR. Because of this, life-changing sporting events have slipped into oblivion. Keeping abreast of the changes in the U.S. Savings Bond program will help you keep your Savings Bond investment from the same fate.

_____ Chapter 15

COMPARATIVE STUDY:
OLD RULES vs. NEW RULES

▸ *Which Bonds Are Affected and What Time Periods Are Covered?*
▸ *Brief Summary of Old Rules*
▸ *Brief Summary of New Rules*
▸ *Impact on:*
   — *Bonds Held Less than Five Years*
   — *Bonds Held More than Five Years*
   — *Educational Savings*
   — *Maturity Periods*
▸ *What Did Bond Owners Lose Under the New Rules?*
▸ *What Did Bond Owners Gain Under the New Rules?*
▸ *GATT-cha: Two Ways the Government is Saving Money*

Tradition.... The fiddler on the roof must have shed a few tears as the Savings Bond program sang its final song eliminating a fifty-year tradition. Effective May 1, 1995, there ceased to be a guaranteed (fixed) interest rate for new purchases of Series EE Bonds. Is this change good or bad for Bond owners?

Which Bonds are Affected and
What Time Periods are Covered?

The only Bonds affected by the new rules are Series EE Bonds. *Series E, H, HH, and Savings Notes are not impacted nor are Series EE Bonds purchased prior to May 1, 1995.* Thus when the term "New Rules" is used, this will apply only to Series EE Bonds purchased May 1, 1995, and after.

Brief Summary of Old Rules

Series EE Bonds purchased from March 1, 1993, to April 30, 1995, receive a flat annual guaranteed rate of 4% if held for less than five years. If held five years or longer, these Bonds will receive the average of the all the long-term variable rates published since the date of purchase or 4%, whichever produces a greater redemption value. At year five, if the average of the long-term rate is higher than 4%, then the average is taken retroactive to date of purchase and compounded forward. This would result in a significant jump in the value of the Bond once held five years.

Brief Summary of New Rules

Series EE Bonds purchased May 1, 1995, and after will have only one rate assigned to them at any given point in time. For the first five years, a new short-term variable rate, which is based on 85% of the average yield for six-month Treasury Bills, will be assigned to each Bond every six months. This rate will be published by the government every May and November. Once a Bond is held five years, a long-term variable rate will be assigned to each Bond every six-month period for as long as the Bond is held, up to year seventeen. After year seventeen, the Bonds can be subjected to different rules at the discretion of the Treasury. The long-term variable rate will be based on the average yield for five-year Treasury Securities. Based on data since 1982, the long-term rate has always been higher than the short-term rate. These Bonds will increase in value semi-annually, on the date of purchase and six months later.

Impact on Bonds Held Less than Five Years

Under the market conditions in effect as of May 1, 1995, the new rules do look more attractive than the old rules. The first short-term variable rate published was 5.25%. That represents a 31% increase above the flat rate of 4% that a Bond owner would have received under the old rules.

Will the new rules always be better for short-term Bond holders? That depends on market conditions. If interest rates remain relatively flat, Bond owners can expect an annual return of 4.5-5.5% for the first five years they hold their Bond—approximately a 25% increase over the rate the old rules would give them. However, if interest rates head south, as they did in 1992-93, the 4% guarantee that was lost might look a lot more important. Suppose the new rules were in effect during 1993—we would have seen a short-term rate as low as 2.58%.

For example, had the new rules been in effect for the five years previous to May 1, 1995, you would have seen the following ten rates applied to your Bond holdings, one for every six-month period.

Table 15.1   # Short-Term Rates 1990-1994

*Please note: The government did not publish a short -term rate until May/1995. Table calculations based on historic data.

Date	Short-Term Rate
May/90	6.63
November/90	6.19
May/91	4.98
November/91	4.44
May/92	3.39
November/92	2.61
May/93	2.58
November/93	2.64
May/94	3.20
November/94	4.34

As you can see these rates would have ranged from a low of 2.58% to a high of 6.63%. Overall, the rates would have averaged 4.1% during this time period. This is well below the 6% guarantee in effect in 1990. And it is only slightly better compared to the most recent guaranteed rate of 4% under the old rules.

Impact on Bonds Held More than Five Years

There is no longer a retroactive feature of the long-term variable rate. One of the little known, very confusing, yet tremendously beneficial features of the old rules was that the long-term variable rate was averaged and applied retroactively to Bonds once the Bond had been held five years. This would be beneficial at best, or have no impact at worst, at the five-year mark. However, as we see in Chapter 3, a long-term retroactive feature can be both confusing and damaging to a Bond owner.

Consider this example: A Bond purchased March 1993 has a guaranteed rate of 4% for the first five years. Over this same five year period ten long-term variable rates will be published. Suppose the average of those ten rates is 6.1%. What would that person actually receive for their Bond? If they cashed in at the 4½-year mark, they would receive only 4% annually for their Bonds. However, once held five years, they receive the 6.1% retroactive to date of purchase and compounded forward. The result is a dramatic increase in the yield for the Bond at the end of year five.

Under the new rules the interest you begin to earn after five years is based on the long-term rate published at that time. This will impact the Bond for a six month period only, the rate is not applied retroactively at all.

Impact on Educational Savings

The new rules have no impact on any of the guidelines or rules covering the educational feature of the EE Bond. Those rules are outlined in Chapter 9. However, the new rules will impact the return a Bond owner receives. (See the impact of new rules for Bonds held less than five years outlined earlier in this chapter, or GATT-cha later in this chapter.)

Impact on Maturity Periods

Series EE Bonds purchased as of May 1, 1995, have an original maturity period of seventeen years. The Bond can reach face value in less than seventeen years, but the original maturity period will remain at seventeen years (see Chapter 4, for further explanation of maturity periods). The first extended maturity period will be ten years and the final extended maturity period will be three years. The Bond will earn interest for a total of thirty years from the date of purchase.

What Did Bond Owners Lose Under the New Rules?

1. *Money*. In most cases, the new rules will pay out less for Bonds held five years or longer. At the five-year mark, your return will be based on rates that have historically averaged 1.5% below the long-term rates that would have been applied retroactively to the date

of purchase under the old rules. (See "GATT-cha", later in this chapter.)

2. *Complexity.* The new rules will be easier to follow. Every six months you pick up a new rate based on current market conditions. Many financial professionals have compared the new rules to continuously rolling over a six-month Certificate of Deposit. This means each time your Bond increases in value, that value is locked in and becomes the base upon which the next increase will be added.

3. *Monthly Increases.* Under the purchase rules in effect from March/1993 to April/1995, Bonds will increase in value monthly for the first five years. Thus you could never forfeit more than one month of interest when redeeming your Bond. The new rules return to a semi-annual increase pattern. Watch those increase dates: Now you can forfeit up to six months of interest if you redeem at the wrong time.

4. *The Guaranteed Floor.* Under the old rules, you have the downside protection of the guaranteed rate (4%). Under the new rules you could be in a free-fall situation.

What Did Bond Owners Gain Under the New Rules?

1. Under the market conditions in effect when the first short-term variable rate was published, Bond owners will receive a more attractive yield under the new rules if they hold the Bonds less than five years. If a Bond is held six months, under the old rules the Bond owner would have received 4%. Under the new rules, if you purchase between May 1, 1995, and October 31, 1995 you will receive 5.25% for the first six-month period.

2. One of the greatest features of the new rules is that Bond owners will be able to clearly understand what the next increase for their Bond will be. The old rules made predicting Bond values very difficult due to the fact that two rates were tracked (guaranteed and variable; see Chapter 3 for additional explanation) and the variable rate had an averaging/retroactive feature. The ability to track and predict future values will aid Bond owners with buying and selling decisions.

3. Under the new rules Series EE Bonds are now guaranteed to reach face value in seventeen years or less, instead of the eighteen years or less under the old rules.

4. Under the new rules, the previous value of a Bond cannot be diluted by falling interest rates. Your Bond will hold its redemption value and will always be credited with the applicable short or long-term variable rate for the next six-month period. Many Bond owners do not realize that the old rules, which have a retroactive feature, can result in net yields for a given period that are less than the

guaranteed rate. (This is because you were previously credited with yields greater than the guaranteed rate.)

GATT-cha: Two Ways the Government is Saving Money

How did the government make money from these changes? Two of the changes, returning to a semi-annual increase and eliminating the retroactive feature of the long-term variable rate, will result in substantial savings for the Treasury Department. A third change, implementing the market-based short-term variable rate, may produce additional savings under specific market conditions.

Return to Semi-Annual Increase Periods

Throughout the history of the Savings Bond program the increase dates have almost always been semi-annual. Only for brief time periods have new issues of Bonds increased in value monthly: that is, until March 1993. Beginning March 1, 1993, new issues of EE Bonds, once held six months, increase in value monthly until the fifth year. With a monthly increase, Bond owners who redeem Bonds cannot forfeit more than thirty days of interest. (If you cash a Bond on the 31st of the month, you will miss the increase that would have been credited to your Bond the first business day of the following month.) By returning to a semi-annual increase, Bond owners can now forfeit up to six months of interest if they do not properly time their redemption.

Potential Savings: To project the savings the following assumptions are made on sales and redemptions. Obviously the savings could be more or less than the projections depending on the actual sales, redemption, and interest figures.

Assumptions:
1. Annual Savings Bond sales will be $10 billion.
2. For a given sales year, Bond owners will redeem 20% ($2 billion) of their purchases within the first five years.
3. Randomly redeeming Bonds will result in an average forfeiture of three months of interest.
4. Short-term variable rates average 5% over a five-year period.

The savings for one year of sales, over a five-year holding/redeeming period, would be $25 million. Thus, five years of sales, with a five-year holding/redeeming period for each sales year, would produce a savings of $125 million.

Keep in mind that over the history of the Bond program semi-annual increases have been the norm, not the exception. The new rules reestablish what has been a history of the program.

Elimination of the Retroactive Feature of Long-Term Market Rate

The second money saver is certainly the most substantial. The new rules eliminate a retroactive feature of the long-term variable rate. Under the old rules, if you hold a Bond five years, you receive either the guaranteed rate or the average of ten long-term variable rates that have been published during the five-year holding period. Bonds purchased in March of 1993 will reach the five-year mark in March of 1998. At the time of writing the average of the long-term rates for these Bonds is 5.17%, while the guaranteed rate for these same Bonds is 4%. If this average holds constant, 5.17% will be applied retroactively to date of purchase after the Bond is five years old. The result will be a significant jump in value.

The new rules assign a different short-term variable rate every six months for the first five years. After five years a long-term rate will be assigned to the Bond for each six-month period. There is no retroactive or lookback feature under the new rules. Historically since the long-term rate has averaged approximately 1.56% higher than the short-term rate, the new rules should produce a tidy savings.

For example: If a $200 Bond purchased May 1, 1995, has short-term variable rates that average 5% over the first five years, the value of a Bond at year five would be $128.01. This would be the value of the Bond under the new rules. Under the old rules, the long-term variable rates would be averaged over the five-year holding period and applied retroactively to date of purchase. Since long-term rates have averaged a full 1½% higher over the last thirteen years, we will make a conservative assumption that the long-term variable rate average is only 1% higher, 6% at year five. Under the old rules this would produce a redemption value of $134.38. The difference on a $100 purchase ($200 Bond) is $6.37. A modest savings for Uncle Sam. Except—when we apply the cumulative impact of this change, the dollars are quite significant.

Potential Savings: If $10 billion of U.S. Savings Bonds are purchased annually, and $8 billion are still being held at the five-year date, the savings of a one percentage point difference (between the long-term rate average and the short-term rate average) will result in approximately $510 million less that the government has to pay out to Bond owners for each purchase year. This is by far the most substantial source of savings that the new rules produced.

Short-Term Market Rate

The final money saver for Uncle Sam will only be realized under certain market conditions, such as those in 1992 and 1993. Removing the guaranteed rate means there is no limit to how low interest rates can go. As you can see from Table 15.1, interest rates in 1992 and 1993 would have produced short-term rates as low as 2.58%. That means Uncle Sam can pay out less than the old rules—with their 4% floor—would have mandated.

For example, suppose you purchased a $1,000 Bond in May 1990. Table 15.2 compares the return under the new and old rules.

Columns B and D are the two values that have been tracked under the old rules for this Bond. The Bond owner automatically receives the rate that produces the highest redemption value once the Bond is held five years: in this case, column B based on the 6% guaranteed rate for this Bond.

If this Bond was governed by the new rules, the value in column F would apply. Due to the lower short-term rates assigned to the Bond, the redemption value at year five is substantially lower than the value produced by the guaranteed rate in column B.

Table 15.2
What If The New Rules Had Been in Effect since 1990?

	A	B	C	D	E	F
Bond Held Five Years: Rates Applied Over Five Year Period	Guaranteed Rate	Value of Bond Based on Column A Interest Rates	Average of Long-Term Variable Rate Retroactive to Purchase Date	Value of Bond Based on Column C Interest Rates	If There Had Been A Short-Term Rate, This Is What It Would Have Been	Value of Bond Based on Column E Interest Rates
		$500.00		$500.00		$500.00
	6.00		5.74		6.63	$516.58
Year 1	6.00		5.74		6.19	$532.56
	6.00		5.74		4.98	$545.82
Year 2	6.00		5.74		4.44	$557.94
	6.00		5.74		3.39	$567.40
Year 3	6.00		5.74		2.61	$574.80
	6.00		5.74		2.58	$582.22
Year 4	6.00		5.74		2.64	$589.90
	6.00		5.74		3.20	$599.34
Year 5	6.00	$671.96	5.74	$663.53	4.34	$612.35

Obviously European wine prices were not the only thing impacted by the GATT legislation..The new rules are easier to track and understand, but they came with a definite cost.

Old rules and new rules, it can be confusing. If you need a customized report that will outline the details for your specific Bonds, contact The Savings Bond Informer, Inc. (See the last page of this book.)

Chapter 16

SUMMARY QUESTIONS, TIPS, AND OPPORTUNITIES

> ▸ *Top Twenty Questions Bond Owners Ask*
> ▸ *Ten Tips for Bond Owners*
> ▸ *A Chance to Become Rich*
> ▸ *A Chance to Become Famous*

Many U.S. Savings Bond owners just do not know where to go to get their questions answered. The Savings Bond Informer, Inc. has assisted thousands of them over the years and has prepared the following summary of the twenty most frequently asked questions. "Ten Tips for Bond Owners" encapsulates the information given in this book. And, to top it all off—a test to demonstrate your new-found knowledge.

Top Twenty Questions Bond Owners Ask

1. *What is the interest rate of Bonds purchased today (May/1995)?*

The only Bond that can be purchased for cash today is the Series EE Bond. As of May 1, 1995, the first short-term variable rate assigned to this Bond is 5.25%. That rate will be in effect for the first six months you hold your Bond and a new rate will be assigned to your Bond every six months. For the current short-term interest rate that applies to new purchases of Series EE Bonds, call 1-800-4USBOND. If you hold your Series EE Bonds at least five years, you become eligible for the long-term variable rate which will generally be higher than the short-term variable rate. (See Chapter 3, "Understanding Interest Rates.")

2.   *How long does it take a Bond to reach face value?*

The time it will take a Bond to reach face value is determined by the interest rates assigned to that Bond. A Series EE Bond purchased today is guaranteed to reach face value in seventeen years or less. If the rates assigned to a Bond average 5%, then that Bond will reach face value in about fourteen years. If the rates average 6%, the Bond will reach face value in about twelve years.

Over the life of the program, Bonds have reached face value anywhere from four years, six months to eighteen years. (See Chapter 4, "Timing Issues and Maturity Periods.")

3.   *Do you have to redeem a Bond when it matures?*

There is a difference between original and final maturity. If you mean original maturity, the answer is no. A Series EE Bond purchased today is guaranteed to reach original maturity in seventeen years. However, Series EE Bonds will earn interest for thirty years from the date of purchase. After thirty years they stop earning interest: This is final maturity. When Bonds stop earning interest, you may either redeem them or exchange them for HH Bonds.

There is good reason not to hold your Bonds past final maturity. First, they have stopped earning interest. Second, the IRS rules state that you are required to report the interest income on Bonds when they reach final maturity (unless you exchange for HH Bonds).

4. *I have EE Bonds with my mother as beneficiary. May I take her name off and put my wife on instead?*

Yes, with EE Bonds the owner may remove the beneficiary's name without the beneficiary's consent. You may then add your wife as a co-owner or beneficiary.

The rules are different for the Series E Bonds. For these, a living beneficiary must consent to having his or her name removed.

5. *Should I exchange all my E and EE Bonds for HH Bonds? I am retired and would like the income.*

If your E Bonds have not reached final maturity, you would generally receive a higher overall yield by selectively redeeming some of the E and EE Bonds instead of exchanging all of them for HH Bonds. (This is being written when HH Bonds are guaranteed 4%. When you exchange, the current rate is locked in for the first ten years.) See Chapter 10 for a complete explanation of selective redemption.

6. *I'm sick and tired of the Bond program; everyone I ask gives me a different answer to my question. Doesn't anyone know Bonds?*

This is a very common complaint. The solution lies in locating the best resource. (As outlined in Chapter 2, there are good reasons why banks do not know all the answers about Savings Bonds.) See Chapter 17 for appropriate resources. It may cost you a long distance phone call or some money for a detailed analysis, but accurate information is worth it—*and it is available.*

7. *I have a number of Series EE Bonds purchased in October 1986. Should I cash them and buy new Bonds?*

Probably not. For the time period you purchased there is a guaranteed rate in effect until the Bond reaches original maturity. Bonds purchased in October 1986 have a guaranteed rate of 7.5% for the first ten years. The Bonds will then enter the next ten-year period with the current guaranteed rate in effect at that time (currently 4%). The Bonds also have an upside potential with the average variable interest rate. The average variable interest rate only affects the Bond if the rate produces a higher redemption value than the guaranteed rate. As for cashing your current EE Bonds and purchasing new EE Bonds, you would be trading Bonds that currently pay 7.5% for Bonds that pay about 5%. You would also have to report all the interest income on the EE Bonds you are cashing. See Chapter 6 for information on how to track your Savings Bond investment.

8. *I should be buying Bonds every chance I get because they are all tax-free for education, right?*

Not exactly. You must meet all the guidelines that apply to this program in order to be eligible. Refer to Chapter 9 for a complete list of the guidelines.

9. *I'm buying Bonds to use for my daughter's college education. I meet the guidelines for the tax-free feature, but if I use the Bonds for her, can I still claim her as a dependent?*

If you buy Series EE Bonds as of January 1, 1990, you may qualify for the educational tax-free status. Taking advantage of the tax-free aspect of EE Bonds when used for college does not affect your right to claim your child as a dependent.

10. *Can a financial institution charge a fee to issue, redeem, or reissue a Savings Bond?*

No, no, and yes. The Treasury Department pays financial institutions for issuing and redeeming Bonds. However, banks do not receive payment for completing reissue forms. Each bank has its own policy regarding fees they charge for reissue transactions, but it is legal for a bank to charge a fee to process your reissue request. See Chapter 11, "Reissuing U.S. Savings Bonds," for additional information.

11. *Over the last twenty years, I have purchased hundreds of Bonds through payroll deduction. I want to trade them all for a few larger denominations. Can I do this?*

There are a couple of considerations here. If you want to exchange for HH Bonds, you can do it with all or a few of your Bonds. However, that may not be the best thing to do considering that HH Bonds are paying only 4% (at the time of writing) and some of your E and EE Bonds are paying a much higher rate.

If you were hoping to exchange or reinvest into EE Bonds of a larger denomination, the answer is a little more complicated. You cannot exchange E or EE Bonds for other EE Bonds. The process would be a redemption (cash in your old Bonds) and a purchase (buy new EE Bonds). This is unattractive for several reasons. Redeeming your old Bonds would mean that you have to report all the interest you have earned on the Bonds to date. Once again, many of these older Bonds are earning an interest rate that is more attractive than the current short-term variable rate on new EE Bonds.

Even though you have a number of Bonds, as long as they are still earning interest you are better off keeping them rather than entering a mass repurchasing program under the current interest rate conditions. One possible exception is your Bonds that have entered extended maturity periods at 4%. Chapter 6 "Tracking Your Investment" provides information on how to determine the interest rates your Bonds are earning. Chapter 10, "Exchanging for HH Bonds," provides additional information.

12. *I am going to buy a used car. I have $4,000 (face value) of Series E Savings Bonds. In order to get the loan, I am going to leave my Bonds with the car dealership as collateral. Are there any problems with this?*

If the dealer takes your Bonds, there is a problem that he does not see. Bonds cannot be transferred or used as collateral, so they are totally worthless to the dealer. Also, keep in mind that depending on the issue date, those E Bonds are worth somewhere between two to six times the face value. That means your Bonds are worth somewhere between $8,000 and $24,000. Forget that used car dealer and head over to the new car lot. But first get an accurate value of your Bonds. Chapter 17 provides a list of resources that will help you to do this.

13. *I purchased Series EE Bonds in the 1980s and was planning to exchange them for HH Bonds. Now that the guaranteed rate has been lowered and I will only be receiving 4% interest, I am not so sure that I want to do this. My Bonds have not matured. Why do Bonds have to be held to maturity before they can be exchanged?*

They don't. Series EE Bonds may be exchanged for HH Bonds anytime after they are six months old. Sorry, but you missed the boat on this one. If you exchanged prior to March 1, 1993, you would have locked in at the old 6% rate. The most probable reason for this misconception is that the two alternatives presented at final maturity are redemption or exchange. The exchange option, which is rarely explained, exists from the time the Bonds are six months old until one year past final maturity.

14. *My uncle and aunt were listed on their Bonds as co-owners. My uncle died first and then my aunt. Who is entitled to the Bonds?*

The estate of the last deceased co-owner.

15. *My wife and I recently created a trust and we want to reissue our Bonds into it. Will this create any tax consequences and what do I need to do?*

If you are co-owners of the Bonds and are also trustees of the trust, and the Social Security number that is on the Bonds is also used for the trust, then you can have your Bonds reissued into the trust without creating a taxable event. You need to complete the PD F 1851. This form is available at your regional Federal Reserve Bank (FRB). There are some cases in which reissuing Bonds into a trust will create a taxable event. See Chapter 8 for more information on tax issues and Chapter 17 for the address and phone number of your regional FRB.

16. *How long does it take to get a response from the Bureau of the Public Debt (BPD)?*

If the request is for forms, they are usually mailed within one to three working days. If the inquiry is for researching lost Bonds, it can take up to a month or more depending on how thoroughly the form was completed. The BPD handles thousands of requests from all over the country. It may take longer than you would like, but they will respond.

17. *Are Bond redemption tables free?*

That depends on which tables you mean. The basic version of the redemption table from the BPD is free. While this table provides values for the lowest denomination Bonds, you must multiply that value by the correct multiple for your Bond. An expanded redemption table which lists the values for all denominations and does not require calculations on the part of the user is available from:

> Superintendent of Documents
> P.O. Box 371954
> Pittsburgh, PA 15250-7954

An annual subscription is $5.00 (price subject to change). For Series E, ask for TRVE; for Series EE, ask for TRVEE. (TRV stands for Table of Redemption Values; E or EE indicates the series.)

18. *Are Bonds a good short-term investment?*

The new rules effective May 1, 1995, actually make Bonds a more attractive short-term investment under current market conditions. The old rules offered a flat guaranteed interest rate of 4% for the first five years. The new rules will assign a new rate to your Bond every six months, tied to the yield of six-month Treasury Bills. The first rate published under the new rules was 5.25% on May 1, 1995. Call 1-800-USBONDS for rates on new purchases.

19. *I received a $200 Series EE Bond last year (1994) when I bought an appliance. They advertised "buy this appliance and get a $200 Bond." Is my Bond worth $200?*

Ah, advertising. All Series EE Bonds are purchased for one-half of the face value. Your "$200" Bond is worth the purchase price of $100, plus one year of interest—about $4. At the guaranteed rate of 4%, it will take eighteen years for your Bond to reach the face value of $200. This is why many companies like to use Bonds for promotions. Ask the merchant for the $200 instead of the $200 Bond.

20. *When will the guaranteed interest rate change again?*

That is a good question. Although the new rules for the Savings Bond program that were implemented May 1, 1995, eliminated the guaranteed rate for new purchases of Series EE Bonds, there is still a guaranteed interest rate on most older Bonds and new issues of HH Bonds. Since major changes to the Bond program were implemented May 1, 1995, it is doubtful that the guaranteed rate will be changed anytime soon. If the market rates stay relatively flat, do not expect to see the guaranteed rate change for a long time. Even if interest rates start to rise, historically the Bond program has lagged behind in making a change to the guaranteed rate.

Ten Tips for Bond Owners

Here is all the information in this book boiled down to the ten most important things Bond owners should know.

1.   Do not rely on verbal information from banks, relatives, or co-workers. Get the facts in writing.

2.   Organize your Bond holdings: You should keep your Bonds and Bond record together in a safe location. An additional copy of the Bond record should be kept in a separate location. The Bond record should contain the serial number, issue date, series, denomination, Social Security number of owner, and registration (names on Bond).

3.   Do not randomly cash your Bonds. Consider the timing issues, interest rates, and tax impact when making your decision.

4.   Do not assume that older Bonds should be cashed first. Obtain the details on each Bond you own and compare one Bond to the next.

5.   Make sure your Bonds have not reached final maturity, at which point they cease to earn interest.

6.   File a PD F 1048 if you have Bonds that have been lost, stolen, or ruined so that your holdings can be researched and, if warranted, replaced.

7.   Do not assume that all your Bonds will become tax-free if used for education. Read the guidelines to determine whether you will be eligible.

8. If you own Bonds that carry the name of a deceased co-owner or beneficiary, have the Bonds reissued. The deceased person's name can be removed and a co-owner or beneficiary of your choosing added. Use form PD F 4000.

9. Do not be misled into thinking that older Bonds (purchased prior to May 1, 1995) are automatically earning the long-term variable rate published every May and November. That rate is never significant by itself. It will become part of an average that may or may not impact your Bond after five years.

10. Save, save, save. U.S. Savings Bonds may not be the greatest investment product in the world, but they are better than some. Millions of Americans have used Bonds to effectively save for the future, purchase cars and homes, or pay for education. Before you invest in any product, obtain current interest rate information.

A Chance to Become Rich

Are you an expert on Savings Bonds now? It is time to test your Savings Bond savvy. If you like a challenge, correctly answer the following questions and you could qualify to win a Savings Bond to add to your holdings (okay, it won't *exactly* make you rich).

List your answers on a postcard (phone calls will not be accepted) and include your name, address, phone number and the phrase "Second Edition, Quiz Answers". Only one entry per person, please. Send the post card to:

The Savings Bond Informer, Inc.
P.O. Box 9249
Detroit, MI 48209

One winner will be chosen every six months (June and December through 1996) and will receive a $50 U.S. Savings Bond. In the event that more than one person answers all of the questions correctly, a drawing will be held to select the winner.

Test

1. Which Series E U.S. Savings Bond will reach final maturity first? A Bond purchased...

    a. February/1959
    b. June/1962
    c. October/1965
    d. January/1967

2. *A Series EE U.S. Savings Bond purchased in 1982 will earn interest for...*

    a. 10 years
    b. 25 years
    c. 30 years
    d. 40 years

3. *All Bonds that are thirty months or older and purchased prior to March 1, 1993, increase in value...*

    a. daily
    b. monthly
    c. quarterly
    d. semi-annually
    e. annually

4. *All Bonds...*

    a. earn the same rate of interest
    b. increase in value at the same time
    c. both a & b
    d. none of the above

5. *When cashing a Bond you will always...*

    a. get the same amount on the twentieth day of the month that you would have received on the first day of the month
    b. get the same amount for each Bond
    c. have a relative asking you for part of the money (even though this may be your experience, this is not the correct answer for everyone)
    d. none of the above

6. *There is one company that created and produces a customized Bond report. This report includes the details for each Bond you own. This company is...*

    a. The Savings Bond Informer, Inc.
    b. The Federal Reserve Bank
    c. Your local bank
    d. Your brother-in-law's barber shop

A Chance to Become Famous

Do you have a Savings Bond question that you would like to see addressed in a future edition of this book? Please send your question to The Savings Bond Informer, P.O. Box 9249, Detroit, MI 48209, Attention: Author.

There are no promises, but if your question would apply to many Bond owners, covers an important topic, or, especially, if it stumps the staff, the answer will be researched and printed in an upcoming edition of the book. If the question is put into print, you will be notified and sent a copy of the answer. Due to the large volume of mail received, a response will be sent only if the question is going to be used in print.

Do you have a Savings Bond story? We would love to hear it and consider it for our next edition.

Services offered by The Savings Bond Informer are on a fee basis only. Letter writers requesting a response for a free consultation will be mailed a brochure outlining the priced services available.

_____

_____ Chapter 17

U.S. SAVINGS BOND RESOURCES

> ▸ *Organizations that Perform Savings Bond Services*
> ▸ *Common Savings Bond Activities: Who Do You Call?*
> ▸ *Forms, Publications, Tables, and How to Get Them*

Doesn't anybody know anything about U.S. Savings Bonds? It seems like I have called all over and every person gives me a different answer!
—A frustrated Bond owner

Every week the author's office receives calls that echo these sentiments. Bond owners are often frustrated, angry, and perplexed as to why they have called all over and cannot get answers to their questions.

There is good news for those people: Many government agencies and a few private companies work exclusively with U.S. Savings Bonds. If you look in the right places, you will find people who do know Bonds and who can answer your questions. If you are treated discourteously or unprofessionally by anyone at any of the resources listed, ask to speak to the supervisor. These specific organizations want to provide quality customer service; if they are not meeting that goal, management would like to know.

This chapter is intended to guide you to the most established and reliable sources of Savings Bond information. The resources listed range from information tables for the do-it-yourselfer to full-service companies that will analyze your Bond holdings for you. The first section lists the organizations, what they do, and how to contact them. The next section lists Savings Bonds activities and assigns the appropriate resource(s) to each. Finally, a listing of Savings Bond publications is given, with ordering information.

Organizations that Perform Savings Bond Services

Government

The Bureau of the Public Debt (BPD): There are two major offices within the BPD: the U.S. Savings Bond Marketing Office and the U.S. Savings Bond Operations Office.

U.S. Savings Bond Marketing Office:

Department of the Treasury
Bureau of the Public Debt
U.S. Savings Bond Marketing Office
Washington, DC 20226

The purpose of this office is to promote the sale and retention of U.S. Savings Bonds. Formerly known as "The Savings Bond Division," this office handles government responsibilities for the annual Savings Bond drive campaign activities. It also handles many of the press releases and media contacts for changes in the Bond program.

U.S. Savings Bond Operations Office:

Bureau of the Public Debt
U.S. Savings Bond Operations Office
PO Box 1328
Parkersburg, WV 26106-1328
(304) 480-6112

At the operations center, hundreds of activities critical to the Bond program are maintained and performed. The Bureau has several "Bond consultants" staffing phones each day from 8:00 a.m. to 4:30 p.m. Eastern Standard Time, Monday through Friday. The Bond consultants are well-versed in a variety of Savings Bond issues and can answer questions or, at least, point you in the right direction. Unfortunately, they do not have an 800 number for the general public. The number listed previously will put you into their automated answering system. At the time this book was written, the menu options were:

2. Nonreceipt of H or HH Bond interest payment
3. To order current redemption tables
4. Current market-based interest rate and maturity period
5. Lost, stolen, or destroyed Bonds
6. Educational Savings Bond program
7. Forms to process a Savings Bond transaction
8. Check the status of a transaction or speak with a Bond consultant
*. Repeat the list of topics
0. Mailing address

If you call after normal business hours, the menu will allow you to access only selection #4 above.

This is one government agency that the author has used extensively. They are taxed with thousands of calls each month, so it can be difficult to get through. Be persistent, though—the staff is knowledgeable and helpful.

Federal Reserve Banks (FRB):

> As fiscal agents of the United States, Federal Reserve Banks and Branches (FRB) perform a number of activities in support of the Savings Bond program, including issuing, redeeming, and reissuing Savings Bonds and Notes. In recent years, both the Bureau of the Public Debt and Federal Reserve Offices have recognized that there would be benefits associated with consolidating certain Saving Bond activities...
>
> —Department of Treasury, BP D, Part 353, 3-80, 6th Amendment (3-4-94).

Please note: As this book was being written, the consolidation was still in process in some regions. That means that some states are already sending their work to the regional sites, while others are scheduled to convert in the near future. If you plan to mail something directly to a FRB, it is best to call your designated site for instructions.

To help point you to the correct FRB, here is the list of consolidated sites as explained in the above publication:

Federal Reserve Bank
Buffalo Branch
P.O. Box 961
Buffalo, NY 14240
(716) 849-5165

This office serves the reserve districts of New York and Boston. The geographic region served includes the following states or portions of states and/or territories: CT, MA, ME, NH, NJ (northern half), NY (city & state), RI, VT, Puerto Rico, and Virgin Islands.

Federal Reserve Bank of Kansas City
P.O. Box 419440
Kansas City, MO 64141-6440
(816) 881-2919 This number will also service Spanish-speaking customers

This office serves the reserve districts of Dallas, San Francisco, Kansas City, and St. Louis. The geographic region served includes the following states or portions of states and/or territories: AK (northern half), AR, AZ, CA, CO, HI, ID, IL (southern half), IN (southern half), KS, KY (western half), LA (northern half), MO, MS, NE, NM, NV, OK, OR, TN (western half), TX, WA, WY, UT, and GU.

Federal Reserve Bank of Minneapolis
250 Marquette Ave.
Minneapolis, MN 55480
(612) 343-5300

This office serves the reserve districts of Minneapolis and Chicago. The geographic region served includes the following states or portions of states: IA, IL (northern half), IN (northern half), MI, MN, MT, ND, SD, WI.

Federal Reserve Bank
Pittsburgh Branch
P.O. Box 299
Pittsburgh, PA 15230-0299
(412) 261-7900

This office serves the reserve districts of Cleveland and Philadelphia. The geographic region served includes the following states or portions of states: DE, KY (eastern half), NJ (southern half), OH, PA, WV (northern panhandle).

Federal Reserve Bank of Richmond
P.O. Box 27622
Richmond, VA 23261
(804) 697-8370

This office serves the reserve districts of Richmond and Atlanta. The geographic region served includes the following states or portions of states: AL, DC, FL, GA, LA (southern half), MD, MS (southern half), NC, SC, TN (eastern half), VA, WV (except northern panhandle).

This office also has a very useful book on Treasury Securities. *Buying Treasury Securities*, Sixteenth Edition, is available by sending $4.50 (check or money order) to the following address:

Buying Treasury Securities
Public Affairs
Federal Reserve Bank of Richmond
P.O. Box 27471
Richmond, VA 23261

Allow four to six weeks for processing.

Nongovernment

Commercial Banks: Thousands of commercial banks provide a variety of services related to the Savings Bond program. The level of service will vary from bank to bank. A thorough description of the bank's relationship to the Bond program is discussed in Chapter 2, "Banks and Bonds: The Untold Story." Here is a summary of the highlights:

✓ U.S. Savings Bonds are not a bank product.
✓ Many banks act as issuing and paying agents for the government (that means they take applications to sell Bonds and they redeem Bonds).
✓ Surveys indicate that they are not a reliable source of information for questions that deal with analyzing Bonds, such as interest rates and timing issues.
✓ Many banks assist Bond owners with processing paperwork when seeking to reissue or exchange Savings Bonds.
✓ The bank expertise related to Savings Bonds is in the area of processing a transaction (a purchase application or a request to redeem Bonds), not in the area of advice or analysis.

The author's travels take him throughout the United States presenting seminars on U.S. Savings Bonds to financial professionals. In each city he makes it a point to visit several banks and ask questions. Time and time again, he has found that tellers confidently provide misinformation on interest rates and timing issues. In fact, they usually consult the redemption tables whether the question is redemption-related or not. Unfortunately, most tellers try to help by suggesting a call to 1-800-USBONDS. You are given the impression that this line is staffed by a real, live person who can answer all the questions that the teller could not. In reality, this 800 number connects you to a recorded message.

National Bond & Trust, Co. (NBT)

National Bond & Trust, Co.
P.O. Box 846
Crown Point, IN 46307
(800) 426-9314

NBT supplies a full range of support services to companies that would like to start a payroll deduction program and those that would like to consider service alternatives for the program they already have.

This company has carved out a unique niche in the marketplace. They essentially do what the government does in terms of conducting a Bond drive. However, as a private company, they add additional elements of service and product to the mix. Here is a list of the services NBT offers.

- Conduct an annual Savings Bond drive
- Maintain records for employees who are buying Bonds through payroll deduction
- Effect all service work needs, such as changes of address, beneficiary or deduction for Bond purchases
- Maintain accurate records of all Bond-related transactions
- Upon request, furnish employer a computer-generated Bond register which reflects individual account status of employee participants

Why is this service being used by numerous companies? Currently many of the above-listed activities are being handled internally by Accounting, Payroll, or Human Resources staff. Staff and computer time cost money. Having an outside source handle many of the administrative aspects of the program can reduce a company's cost of having a Bond program.

They also offer a unique insurance component to participants of the Bond program. This component is not mandatory for the Bond owner. **Important note**: NBT's 800 number is only for businesses who wish to inquire about NBT's services. *This number is not for general information or for answering other Savings Bond questions.*

The Savings Bond Informer, Inc.

The Savings Bond Informer, Inc.
P.O. Box 9249
Detroit, MI 48209
(800) 927-1901 for brochure and description of services

This company was founded by the author in 1990 to service Bond owners and financial professionals whose clients own U.S. Savings Bonds. The primary service of this organization is to create a written report of your Savings Bonds (an alternative to the do-it-yourself tracking of your investment described in Chapter 6). The report contains the specific values, interest rates, timing issues, maturity dates, and extended maturity dates for each Bond a person owns. The fees for a customized report are displayed in Table 17.1 following. (See the form at the back of the book to order.)

Table 17.1

Price List
For a Bond Report

A Bond Report For:	Total Cost
1 to 10 Bonds	$12.00
11 to 25 Bonds	$19.00
26 to 75 Bonds	$29.00
76 to 150 Bonds	$39.00
151 to 300 Bonds	$49.00
301 to 500 Bonds	$69.00
501 to 750 Bonds	$99.00
751 to 1000 Bonds	$129.00
1001 to 1250 Bonds	$159.00
1251 to 1500 Bonds	$189.00

Important note: The Savings Bond Informer, Inc. does provide one free phone consultation for customers who have already ordered a Bond report. **Identifying the account number on your report is necessary for the free phone consultation.** Phone consultations without ordering a report are available from the author for a fee of $35 per fifteen-minute segment (minimum billing $35). Credit card payment is required at the time of call.

Additional services of The Savings Bond Informer, Inc.: Consulting services are provided to banks, corporations, and financial professionals. Consultations include a review of service levels and assesment of potential liabilities, as well as ideas for opportunities to enhance service and create corporate revenue related to the Bond program. Personnel training is available. Fees vary. The Savings Bond Informer, Inc. also conducts seminars for financial professionals throughout the United States.

Other Financial Professionals:

This next category is very difficult to characterize. There are hundreds of specialty areas within each profession. Although a financial professional may be highly trained, often that training has not included a study of U.S. Savings Bonds. This section is not an endorsement nor an indictment of any particular group of financial professionals, but we will attempt to give you some Bond-related background for each.

Accountants: Accountants may be very helpful in evaluating tax issues related to your Bond holdings. If you want to have an accountant evaluate your Bonds, determine a cost for the service ahead of time. A Bond owner in Ohio was surprised to discover that due to the time-consuming nature of tracking a Bond investment, an accountant had charged over $1,000 to value her Bonds. Before you engage the services of an accountant for U.S. Savings Bonds find out if he or she has had previous experience with Bond-related work and what their fee is.

Accountant, professional counsel: Brent Dawes is a C.P.A. who specializes in tax questions, research, and counsel on Savings Bond issues. He is also a contributor to this book (see Chapter 8). His fee is $35 per fifteen minutes, minimum fee $35 (charged to Visa or Mastercard at the time of call). This may be helpful to other financial professionals or Bond owners who have a particular situation that calls for tax advice. The firm is American Express Tax and Business Services, Inc. Their number is 1-800-851-2324. Tell them that you are calling for tax counsel regarding U.S. Savings Bonds.

Attorneys: Many attorneys handle Savings Bond transactions, most commonly for estate settlement or trust purposes. Many law offices use the services of The Savings Bond Informer, Inc. to value Bonds, others calculate the data themselves. Fees vary depending on the complexity of the case and the pricing structure of the individual office.

Financial Planners: It is the author's assessment that a good financial planner will take the time to understand your financial situation and evaluate your status before they offer counsel. Related to Savings Bonds, a planner should be able to provide you with written details about your investment. The written analysis can act as a tool to compare your holdings to other options and contribute to an accurate net worth statement.

Common Savings Bond Activities: Who Do You Call?

The following is a list of common Bond activities. Listed after each activity are the organizations or institutions to contact regarding that particular activity. The address and phone number for many of the organizations can be found in the preceding pages of this chapter.

Buying Bonds

Financial institutions: Most commercial banks still sell U.S. Savings Bonds, but call before you go. In our phone survey of banks, we discovered several banks that no longer sell Bonds. (Some savings & loans and credit unions also sell U.S. Savings Bonds.) The commercial bank will take your application and money and forward it to a regional FRB site for processing.

Federal Reserve Banks: You can mail your application to purchase U.S. Savings Bonds directly to any FRB. The application may be forwarded to another FRB for processing, but your closest FRB will ensure that your application is sent to the correct site. Make your check payable to "The Federal Reserve Bank." Be sure to include your purchase application, completed in full. Also include your telephone number so they can reach you if there are any questions.

Payroll Deduction: To buy Bonds through payroll deduction, your company must have a Payroll Savings Plan in place. Printing and mailing the Bonds is handled at a regional Federal Reserve Bank, another qualified issuing agent, or through another party such as National Bond & Trust. (There are typically no fees charged to deal with any of the organizations; however, the level and type of service they offer may differ).

Redeeming Bonds and Exchanging Bonds

Financial institutions: Most commercial banks will redeem and exchange U.S. Savings Bonds, but, again, call before you go. In our phone survey of banks, we discovered several banks that no longer provided these services. Some savings & loans and credit unions also redeem U.S. Savings Bonds. The commercial bank has a specific set of guidelines to follow when redeeming Bonds. Cases that they are unable to process will be forwarded to the FRB or the BPD. H and HH Bonds are forwarded to the FRB. If you are redeeming less than $1,000 in E or EE Bonds and have proper identification, you should receive your money the same day.

Federal Reserve Banks: FRBs will act as a redemption site for Bond owners, though the request may be forwarded to another FRB for processing. Expect three to five business days for payment. Call for specific instructions from the FRB you intend to use.

Determining the Value of Your Bonds

Author's note: If you have 50 Bonds or more, none of the free services listed below will read off the redemption values over the phone or in person. They will mail you a redemption table and expect you to value the Bonds yourself. Why? Consider it from a bank's perspective. It is Friday afternoon, hundreds of customers are cashing payroll checks, and your needs will consume at least one hour of a teller's time—for which the bank will not make any money. Savvy banks will send you to the customer service area so that their financial representative can pitch their own bank products in exchange for their time. Remember that bank information on Savings Bond interest rates and timing issues is often inaccurate (See Chapter 2).

Commercial Banks (no fee): The level of service here may vary, depending on your customer status. Most banks will provide values for a reasonable number of Bonds without any qualms. Larger number of Bonds may not be serviced for reasons noted above.

Federal Reserve Bank (no fee): FRBs will mail a redemption table to you and may price a couple of Bonds over the phone.

Bureau of the Public Debt (no fee): BPD will mail a redemption table to you.

The Savings Bond Informer, Inc. (fee). TSBI will produce a statement or report of your Savings Bond holdings which includes values as well as interest rates, timing issues, explanation of maturity dates, and accrued interest. You supply the month/year of purchase (issue date), face value, and series. If you have further questions after ordering the report, a free phone consultation is provided. Refer to the prices in Table 17.1.

Tables for Analyzing Bonds On Your Own

There are several current government tables you will need to analyze the details of your Bonds. There is no charge for these tables.

- ✓ Table of Redemption Values for Series E and EE Bonds and SN
- ✓ Guaranteed Minimum Rates Table
- ✓ Semi-annual Interest Rate Bulletin
- ✓ Interest Accrual Dates

Examples of these can be found in Chapter 6, Tables 6.3 through 6.7. Chapter 6 also provides a thorough step-by-step explanation on how to analyze your Bonds and create a Bond statement.

The **FRB** will mail out most of the items while the **BPD** will mail any or all of the items. Contact:

Bureau of the Public Debt
P.O. Box 1328
Parkersburg, WV 26106-1328
(304) 480-6112

Additional note: The Table of Redemption Values provides values for the lowest denomination of Bonds, but you must multiply that value by the correct multiple for your Bond. An expanded redemption table which lists the values for all denominations and does not require calculations on the part of the reader is available from:

Superintendent of Documents
P.O. Box 371954
Pittsburgh, PA 15250-7954

An annual subscription is $5.00 (price subject to change). For Series E, ask for TRVE; for Series EE ask for TRVEE. (TRV stands for Table of Redemption Values; E or EE indicates the series.)

Reissuing Bonds

Federal Reserve Bank: FRB regional sites accept all reissue transactions. Customer service representatives will answer questions related to reissue transactions. Some cases are forwarded to the BPD.

Commercial Banks: Banks may have the forms needed to complete reissue transactions. Some will help you complete the forms, but there may be a fee involved.

Bureau of the Public Debt: (304) 480-6112. Bond consultants staff phones from 8:00 a.m. to 4:30 p.m., EST. All reissue forms may be ordered from the BPD.

Legal Questions

Bureau of the Public Debt: See address listing.

Attorneys: You may also want to consult with an attorney for estate, probate, custody issues, and other legal concerns.

Educational Feature of Bonds

Ask for both the Questions & Answers publication on the educational feature of EE Bonds and the brochure that outlines the guidelines. These are available from:

- ✓ Bureau of the Public Debt
  PO Box 1328
  Parkersburg, WV 26106-1328
- ✓ Federal Reserve Bank Regional Sites
- ✓ Some commercial banks

Lost, Stolen, or Destroyed Bonds

Ask for form PD F 1048, available from:

- ✓ Bureau of the Public Debt
- ✓ Federal Reserve Bank Regional Sites
- ✓ Some commercial banks

Forms, Publications, Tables, and How To Get Them

All of the following forms and regulations are available from the BPD, Savings Bond Operations Office. FRBs will also have most, if not all, of the forms. Many banks stock the forms used most often. Table 17.2 and the following lists are from "The Book on U.S. Savings Bonds" and the brochure "U.S. Savings Bonds, Buyers Guide 1993-94."

Table 17.2

Treasury Circulars

Subject	CFR Part	Treasury Circular
Offering of Series E Bonds	316	No. 653
Offering of Series EE Bonds	351	No. 1-80
Offering of Savings Notes	342	No. 3-67
Offering of Series H Bonds	332	No. 905
Offering of Series HH Bonds	352	No. 2-80
Regulations Governing Series E and H Bonds	315	No. 530
Regulations Governing Series EE and HH Bonds	353	No. 3-80
Regulations Governing Exchange Transactions	352	No. 2-80

Adapted from "The Book on U.S. Savings Bonds,, p.1.

The following is a list of PD forms pertinent to U.S. Savings Bonds and Notes. The government often revises forms to accommodate changes that have occurred in the Bond program. When ordering a form, explain why you need it. That way, if there have been any changes, you will get the most recent and appropriate, form.

PD F 1048
Application for Relief on Account of Loss, Theft, or Destruction of United States Savings and Retirement Securities

PD F 1455
Request by Fiduciary for Reissue of United States Savings Bonds/Notes

PD F 1522
Special Form of Request for Payment of United States Savings Bonds/Notes and Retirement Securities Where Use of a Detached Request is Authorized

PD F 1849
Disclaimer of Consent With Respect to United States Savings Bonds/Notes

PD F 1851
Request for Reissue of United States Savings Bond/Notes in Name of Trustee of Personal Trust Estate

PD F 1938
Request for Reissue of United States Savings Bond/Notes During the Lives of Both Co-owners

PD F 1946
Application for Disposition—United States Savings Bonds/Notes and/or Related Checks (in a Combined Amount Not Exceeding $1,000) Owned by Decedent Whose Estate is Being Settled Without Administration

PD F 1946-1
Application for Disposition—United States Savings Bonds/Notes and/or Related Checks Owned by Decedent Whose Estate is Being Settled Without Administration

PD F 1980
Description of United States Savings Bonds Series H/HH

PD F 1993
Request for Purchase of United States Savings Bonds With Proceeds of Payment of Matured Savings Bonds

PD F 2216
Application by Preferred Creditor for Disposition Without Administration Where Deceased Owner's Estate Includes United States Registered Securities and/or Related Checks in Amount not Exceeding $500

PD F 2458
Certificate of Entitlement—United States Savings and Retirement Securities and Checks After Administration of Decedent's Estate

PD F 2488-1
Certificate by Legal Representative(s) of Decedent's Estates, During Administration, of Authority to Act and of Distribution Where Estate Holds No More Than $1,000 (Face Amount) United States Savings Bonds/Notes, Excluding Checks Representing Interest

PD F 2513
Application by Voluntary Guardian of Incompetent Owner of United States Savings Bonds

PD F 2966
Special Bond of Indemnity to the United States of America

PD F 3062
Claim for Relief on Account of Inscribed United States Savings Bonds Lost, Stolen or Destroyed Prior to Receipt by Owner, Co-owner, or Beneficiary

PD F 3253
Exchange Subscription for United States Savings Bonds or Series HH

PD F 3360
Request for Reissue of United States Savings Bond/Notes in the Name of a Person or Persons Other Than the Owner (Including Legal Guardian, Custodian for a Minor Under a Statute, etc.)

PD F 4000
Request by Owner for Reissue of United States Savings Bonds/Notes to Add Beneficiary or Co-owner, Eliminate Beneficiary or Decedent, Show Change of Name, and/or Correct Error in Registration

PD F 4881
Application for Payment of United States Savings Bonds of Series EE or HH and/or Related Checks in an Amount Not Exceeding $1,000 by the Survivor of a Deceased Owner Whose Estate is Not Being Administered

PD F 5263
Order for Series EE U.S. Savings Bonds (RDS)

PD F 5336
Application for Disposition of United States Savings Bonds/Notes and/or Related Checks Owned by Decedent Whose Estate is Being Settled Without Administration

This resource section should provide you with an organization to contact for virtually any question that was not addressed in this book. Since change is ongoing within the Bond program, you may want to contact the publisher for revised copies of this book in future years.

Glossary

Accrual method (or basis) of income reporting: Income is reported when earned or when the taxpayer has an unrestricted right to the income. The timing of the actual receipt of the income does not matter under this reporting method.

Amended returns: An income tax return filed after the original tax return has been filed to correct or change items filed on the original return. Amended returns can be filed within three years of filing the original return to claim refunds.

Automatic default: The result that will take place if no specific steps are taken to choose another alternative.

Average market-based rate: The rate produced by totaling all the individual market-based rates published during the life of a Bond and then dividing that total by the number of rates. See Variable Interest Rate.

Beneficiary: The person designated as a POD (Pay on Death) on a Savings Bond. This person is entitled to the Bond only upon the death of the first-named party on the Bond.

Bureau of the Public Debt (BPD): Government office that acts under the direction of the Department of Treasury. It has two main functions pertaining to the Bond program: The U.S. Savings Bond Marketing Office promotes the sale and retention of Bonds and the U.S. Savings Bond Operations Office oversees all operational issues related to the Bond program.

Cash method (or basis) of income reporting: Income is reported only when it is actually received, not when it was earned.

197

Current income Bonds: Bonds that produce an interest payment to the Bond owner. H and HH Bonds are examples of current income securities because they pay an interest payment to the Bond owner every six months.

Date of purchase: See Issue Date.

Decedent: The person named on a Bond who is now deceased.

Deferral: Postponing the reporting of the income in a legal manner until a later time.

Denomination: See face value.

Disposition: To transfer or part with by gift or sale.

Extended maturity: The term(s) of life-bearing interest granted to a Bond after the Bond reaches original maturity. It is normally ten years, except for final extension which may be less than ten years.

Exchange for HH Bonds: The process of exchanging Series E or EE Bonds, Savings Notes, or eligible H Bonds for Series HH Bonds.

Face value: The dollar amount printed on the front of the Bond.

Federal Reserve Bank (FRB): "As fiscal agents of the United States, Federal Reserve Banks and Branches (FRB) perform a number of activities in support of the Savings Bond program, including issuing, redeeming, and reissuing Savings Bonds and Notes." (Department of Treasury, BPD, Part 353, 3-80, 6th Amendment, 3-4-94).

Final maturity: The date at which a Bond stops earning interest.

Fixed rate: A rate that does not fluctuate for a designated period of time.

FRB: See Federal Reserve Bank.

Freedom Share: See Savings Notes.

GATT: General Agreement on Trades and Tariffs. Legislation passed by the United States in December 1994.

Guaranteed interest rate: A fixed rate of interest that applies to a Bond in an original maturity period or an extended maturity period. This rate is not tied to any specific market condition and is set at the discretion of the Department of Treasury.

HH direct deposit: For all new issues of HH Bonds, the interest must be directly deposited to an account of the Bond holders choosing. This means that a check is not issued; the money is sent to the designated account on the day the interest is to be paid to the Bond holder.

Interest income: The difference between the purchase price and the redemption value of Series E and EE Bonds and SNs is interest income. For H and HH Bonds, the amount received every six months via check (for older Bonds) or direct deposit is considered interest income in the year in which it is received.

Interest accrual security: A Bond in which the interest is added to the value of the Bond; thus, the Bond increases in value over time.

Issue date: The specific date assigned to a Bond. This appears in the top right-hand corner of each Bond. It will always involve a month and year. This date determines the set of interest rates, values, and timing issues that will apply to a given Bond.

Long-term market rate: Published every May and November. Based on 85% of the average yield of five-year Treasury securities for the six months immediately preceding the month of publication. This rate will only impact Bonds for a given six-month period. It is not averaged with any other long-term rates published for Bonds purchased on or after May 1, 1995, and that are over five years old. This rate is averaged with other long-term rates for Bonds over five years old that were published prior to May 1, 1995.

Maturity periods: Bonds have an original maturity period, extended maturity period, and a final maturity. Each Bond is unique and thus the maturity periods differ for each Bond.

New guaranteed rate: The guaranteed rate most recently assigned to purchases of Series EE Bonds from March 1, 1993 to April 30, 1995 and to Series HH Bonds obtained after February 28, 1993. As of March 1, 1993, the guaranteed rate is 4%. This rate does not impact Series EE Bonds purchased after April 30, 1995.

Nominee: A co-owner of a Bond who redeems the Bond, but is not legally liable for the tax on the interest received because the principal owner is living and the principal owner's funds were used to purchase the Bond.

Original maturity: The time period that it will take for a Bond to reach face value at the guaranteed interest rate in effect at time of purchase, or a set period of seventeen years for Series EE Bonds purchased after April 30, 1995.

Payroll Savings Plan: A program that many companies offer that allows employees the option to have a regular amount deducted from each paycheck to apply to the purchase of Bonds. Also known as payroll deduction and systematic purchase.

PD Forms: Forms issued by the BPD for the purpose of collecting the appropriate information to authorize specific Bond transactions. See Chapter 17 for a listing.

Purchase application: The form a person completes to purchase a Series EE Savings Bond.

Redemption value: The value of a Bond at a given point in time.

Redemption: The act of presenting Bonds for payment.

Regional distribution site: A FRB that has been chosen as one of five sites to service Bond transactions.

Registered security: A Bond that is inscribed with the name or names of persons entitled to the Bond.

Registration: The form of inscription upon a Bond.

Reissue: The act of changing a registration upon a Bond. This can only be done by a FRB or the BPD. A Bond owner can never make marks on a Bond to change the registration of that Bond.

Residuary beneficiaries: The person(s) entitled to assets of an estate after all expenses have been paid by the estate and all assets that were designated to specific individuals have been distributed.

Savings Notes (SN): A Bond also known as the "Freedom Share," it was issued during the Vietnam War era, from May 1967 to October 1970. It is similar to Series E and EE Bonds in that it is an interest accrual Bond. The major difference is that this Bond was purchased for 81% of face value. These Bonds will earn interest for thirty years.

Schedule B: Internal Revenue Service tax form to list itemized deductions.

Selective redemption: The process of specifically choosing one Bond over another to redeem, based on the Bond owner's evaluation of interest rates, timing issues, and maturity dates.

Series E: Commonly referred to as the old "War Bonds" because they were issued to help finance World War II. The first Bonds in this series were issued in May 1941 and the last in June 1980. These Bonds are all worth more than their face value. Bonds issued before December 1965 earn interest for forty years. Bonds issued December 1965 and after earn interest for thirty years.

Series EE: Issued since January 1980 until the present. An interest accrual Bond, the value of the Bond grows over time. It is always purchased for one-half of face value. The time period to original maturity varies from eight to eighteen years, depending on the date of purchase. This series will earn interest for thirty years from date of purchase.

Series H: A current income Bond with a interest-producing life of thirty years. It was issued from June 1952 through December 1979.

Series HH: A current income Bond that can be obtained only by exchanging Series E and EE Bonds and Savings Notes, or through the reinvestment of eligible H Bonds. This Bond produces an interest payment to the Bond owner every six months. It has been available since January 1980.

Series identification: This is the specific series that is printed on the face of the Bond, indicating the type of Bond. The most common Bonds will be one of the following series: Series E, EE, H, HH, or Savings Notes (also known as Freedom Shares).

Short-term market rate: Published every May and November. Based on 85% of the average yield of six-month Treasury Bill yields for the three months immediately preceding the month of publication. This rate will only impact Bonds for a given six-month period. It is not averaged with any other short-term rates published. This applies only to EE Bonds purchased on or after May 1, 1995, and that are less than five years old.

SN: See Savings Notes.

Stepped-up basis: When qualifying assets are inherited, the value of the asset at the original owner's death becomes the basis for determining the gain or loss if the new owner sells the asset. This is called "the basis" from the original cost of the asset to the fair market value in the decedent's estate. U.S. Savings Bonds do not qualify for "stepped-up basis" treatment.

Systematic Purchase: See Payroll Savings Plan.

1099-INT: The form a Bond owner will receive from the redeeming institution when a Bond transaction results in reporting interest income. A copy of the information on this form is also supplied to the Internal Revenue Service.

Timing issues: Bonds are affected by the time periods. Bonds purchased prior to March 1, 1993, (that are at least thirty months old) will increase in value semi-annually. Timing a redemption or exchange to coincide with the increase pattern will result in the Bond owner receiving a greater return on the Bond investment. Another timing concern is the date that a Bond enters an extended maturity period, and being assigned a different guaranteed interest rate. Timing also is a factor when a Bond reaches final maturity as the Bond owner has only one year past final maturity to exchange Bonds.

U.S. Savings Bonds report or statement: A detailed analysis of U.S. Saving Bonds. Bond owners can create this report themselves by following the instructions in Chapter 6 or they can order a report for a fee from The Savings Bond Informer, Inc.

Variable interest rate: Also referred to as the market-based individual variable interest rate, it is published every May 1 and November 1. This rate, when combined with all the other individual variable interest rates published over the life of a Bond, contributes to the average variable interest rate.

Bibliography

Bamford, Janet. "The Class of 2013." *Sesame Street Parents* (September 1994): 52-55.

Nadler, Paul S. "Uncle Sam Out of Line." *Banker's Monthly* 109 (November 1992): 8.

NYNEX Corporation. "U.S. Savings Bonds, 1994 Campaign: Visions of America." New York, NY.

Quinn, Jane Bryant. "Stand by Your Pension: When a company sloughs off an ex-spouse." *Newsweek* CXXIV (4 July 1994): 65.

"Save-Bond." *Associated Press.* (24 August 1994) 2209PDT.

U.S. Department of the Treasury, Bureau of the Public Debt. *31 CFR Part 351, "Public Debt Series No. 1-80; Final Rule."* (March 1995).

U.S. Department of the Treasury, Bureau of the Public Debt. *Federal Register*, vol. 59, pt. 3, "Offering and Governing Regulations for United States Savings Bond; Final Rule." No. 43 (4 March 1994).

U.S. Department of the Treasury, Bureau of the Public Debt. *Federal Register*, vol. 59, "Offering of United States Savings Bonds Series HH." No. 43 (4 March 1994).

U.S. Department of the Treasury, Bureau of the Public Debt. *Federal Register*, vol. 58, pt. 4, "Offering of United States Savings Bonds and United States Savings Notes; Final Rule." No. 221 (18 November 1993).

U.S. Department of the Treasury, Bureau of the Public Debt. *Federal Register*, vol. 55, "Regulations Governing United States Savings Bonds, Series EE and HH." No. 4 (5 January 1990).

U.S. Department of the Treasury, Bureau of the Public Debt, U.S. Savings Bond Division. "A History of the United States Savings Bond Program." Washington, D.C.: Government Printing Office (1991).

U.S. Department of the Treasury, Bureau of the Public Debt, U.S. Savings Bond Division. "Buyer's Guide: 1993-1994." No. SBD-2085. Washington, D.C.: Government Printing Office (1993).

U.S. Department of the Treasury, Bureau of the Public Debt, U.S. Savings Bond Division. "The Savings Bond Question & Answer Book." Washington, D.C.: Government Printing Office (1994).

U.S. Department of the Treasury, Bureau of the Public Debt, U.S. Savings Bond Division. "U.S. Savings Bonds: Now Tax-Free for Education." No. SBD-2017.

U.S. Department of the Treasury, Bureau of the Public Debt, Savings Bond Marketing Division. "The Book on U.S. Savings Bonds." No. SBD-2080. Washington, D.C.: Government Printing Office (1994).

U.S. Department of the Treasury, Bureau of the Public Debt, Savings Bond Marketing Division. "Legal Aspects of United States Savings Bonds" No. SBD-2113. Washington, D.C.: Government Printing Office.

U.S. Department of the Treasury, Internal Revenue Service. "Investment Income and Expenses: For use in preparing 1993 Returns." Pubn. No. 550. Washington, D.C.: Government Printing Office (1994).

U.S. Department of the Treasury, Internal Revenue Service. "Your Federal Income Tax: For use in preparing 1993 Returns." Pubn. No. 17. Washington, D.C.: Government Printing Office (1994).

Index

BOOK ORDER FORM

Telephone Orders: Call Toll Free 800 927-1901. Visa, MasterCard and AMEX accepted.
Fax Orders: 313-843-1912
Postal Orders: TSBI Publishing, P.O. Box 9249, Detroit, MI 48209   313 843-1910

Company (if applicable): _____

"Mail to" Name: _____

Address: _____

_____

City: _____   State: _____   Zip: _____

Please send me:
Number of books requested: _____ x $24.95 = _____

Shipping cost: $3.00 for the first book,
                      $1.00 for each additional book:
                                          Shipping   _____

                Michigan residents only, add 6% sales tax: _____

                              Total Cost: _____

Please make checks payable to: **TSBI Publishing**

Credit card payment: ☐ Visa or ☐ MasterCard ☐ AMEX (check one)

Name on Card _____

Expiration date on card _____/_____ Month/Year

Number on Card _____

Gift Order Form

Please check here _____ if you would like TSBI Publishing to ship the book to someone, as a gift from you. To order the book "U.S. Savings Bonds: A Comprehensive Guide for Bond Owners and Financial Professionals", as a gift for someone else, simply complete the order form above, indicating the name and address you would like the book sent to. We would be happy to enclose a short note, and/or your name along with the book.

This gift is courtesy of: _____

Please include the following note to the recipient of the book:

_____

_____

THANK YOU

The Savings Bond Informer, Inc.
BOND STATEMENT ORDER FORM

Name to appear on Bond Statement:_____

Name of Financial Professional (if applicable)**:** _____

Company (if applicable):_____ **Phone:** _____

"Mail to" Name: _____

Address:_____

City:_____ **State:**_____ **Zip Code:**_____

To receive complete details about each bond, mail a copy of this list, along with your payment, to:

The Savings Bond Informer, Inc. P.O. Box 09249 Detroit, MI 48209	OR	Fax your order: (313) 843-1912 Visa, MasterCard & AMEX accepted

If you have any questions about how to order, call **1-800-927-1901.** The cost for a Savings Bond statement is determined by the number of Bonds included in the statement. All orders are processed within ten days of receipt. Please include your check with your order. For Fax orders include your credit card number and expiration date.

A Bond Statement For:	Total Cost	Check One	
1 to 10 bonds	$12.00		
11 to 25 bonds	$19.00		Enter total number of bonds, as listed below and on attached pages:
26 to 75 bonds	$29.00		
76 to 150 bonds	$39.00		
151 to 300 bonds	$49.00		_____
Over 301 bonds	see page 187, or call for quote		

BOND LIST

Issue Date (Month/Year)	Face Value	Series (E,EE,H,HH,FS)	Issue Date (Month/Year)	Face Value	Series (E,EE,H,HH,FS)

To continue record, attach additional pages (see page 47 for blank "Bond List Sheet"). 16